Your Career In
TRAVEL

ARCO'S
Career
Guidance
Series

Your Career In
TRAVEL

Janet Hollander
and
Joe Hollander

**ARCO PUBLISHING, INC.
NEW YORK**

Published by Arco Publishing, Inc.
219 Park Avenue South, New York, N.Y. 10003

Library of Congress Cataloging in Publication Data

Hollander, Janet.
    Your career in travel.

    (Arco's career guidance series)
    Bibliography: p. 109
    Includes index. 83-4833
    1. Travel agents—Vocational guidance. I. Hollander,
Joseph.   II. Title.   III. Series.
G154.H64   381′.459104′02373   81-7918
ISBN 0-668-05175-2 (Library Edition)   AACR2
ISBN 0-668-05182-5 (Paper Edition)

Printed in the United States of America

CONTENTS

FOREWORD

Travel is certainly a career field full of opportunities. You may get a chance to go anywhere in the world, and you will get an opportunity to work in a dynamic service industry. Whether on a trip or in an office you probably will meet many interesting people who, like you, want the adventure, escape, and variety that the travel experience can bring. Remember, too, that the travel business is growing. There are more and better jobs than ever before, and the prospects for increased growth are good. Today, more people go more places for more reasons than ever before. This means more opportunities for you.

But where are you to find a place in the big, expanding world of the travel business? How can you tell which job will best suit you? *Your Career in Travel* will help you make these decisions by describing possible jobs, telling you what kind of education and training you must have to get such positions, and outlining the chances for you to get promotions, raises, and other benefits from your job. The book also includes chapters to help you evaluate your own talents, interests, and potential, as well as sections that tell you where to go to be trained for travel work. All this will help you get started on the career path that is right for you.

Few people are better equipped to help you decide if the travel industry has a career for you than Janet and Joe Hollander. Mrs. Hollander is a former high school teacher who is now involved in training travel agents. She is currently studying for her Master's degree in Tourism and Travel Administration at the New School for Social Research. Mr.

Foreword

Hollander is an editor and writer who, with his wife, has traveled widely and often. Their backgrounds and experience can also help you to focus *Your Career in Travel.*

Louise Colligan
Director, Education and Training Department
American Society of Travel Agents, Inc.

Your Career In
TRAVEL

1
WHAT IS THE TRAVEL INDUSTRY?

Today, travelers can choose from an enormous number of ways to get places, and they have many more places to go because they can get there so quickly. The travel industry provides all the services that people on the move require. Some industry representatives help plan and arrange trips; others set up and maintain the planes, trains, ships, buses, and cars that carry travelers to their destinations; and still others train, regulate, and supply the industry itself.

In this book we will look at each of these sides of the travel industry, exploring how people get jobs in the field, what they do for their customers, and what they can expect to happen in their own careers and in the industry as a whole over the next few years. But first let's explore some general facts about the travel field.

Why People Travel

Adventure, fun, new sights and sounds are some of the obvious goals of travel — we all want a vacation and time to relax in a pleasant environment. But people also travel to do business, to visit family and friends, to explore new opportunities, and for many, many other reasons. Think of a person you know who is interested in art and who longs to visit a distant museum or the home of a famous painter. Consider the fisherman eager to try a faraway stream, the mountain climber challenged by the Himalayas, the golfer who wants to play the St. Andrews's course in Scotland. And what about people who like to sample new kinds of foods, shop for exotic products, or merely meet new and different people? Curiosity, relaxation,

Adventure, fun, new sights and sounds are some of the obvious goals of travel.

freedom from responsibilities—all prompt us away from our homes and out into the world. This variety of reasons to travel, along with a whole world of places to go and ways to get there, makes the travel industry so big and so complex.

How the Travel Industry Operates

As we mentioned, the travel industry actually is composed of many different businesses and services: travel agents, transportation services, hotels, and the businesses and people that keep these parts of the industry going.

Imagine you are taking a trip to Hawaii. Think of all the people who would work for you as you traveled. First, you probably would take a plane (or perhaps a ship) to Hawaii. But just getting you on the plane requires the efforts of lots of people in the travel industry: a porter meets you at the airline terminal door and checks your baggage or carries it to the proper check-in line. Then another person checks or sells you your ticket, perhaps using a computer. This person assigns you a seat on the plane and tags your baggage or attaches the proper claim tags to your ticket to make sure that your baggage arrives with your flight. Then you go through a security gate, where guards check your hand-carried luggage, and move on to the departure gate, where a ground attendant announces your flight, takes your ticket, and guides you to your plane. While you are boarding the plane, other people are loading your baggage on the plane, inspecting and fueling the aircraft, cleaning cabins, and filling the galleys with meals to be served during the flight. The pilot and cockpit crew are busy checking weather conditions and flight routines, readying the plane for takeoff, and keeping passengers and cabin crew informed about schedules, destinations, and the like. Inside the plane flight attendants greet you and direct you to your seat, providing information about meals, films to be shown enroute, and safety regulations. As the aircraft taxis from the departure gate, air-traffic controllers guide the plane onto runways and through the maze of airport ground and air traffic. Finally, you are airborne! Through just this small portion of your trip, you personally have encountered at least a dozen people doing different jobs to help you on your way. And we have said nothing about the travel agent who helped plan your trip, the service people who got you to the airport, or all the travel industry people waiting for you in Hawaii at such places as hotels, restaurants, and tour agencies.

Let's look briefly at some of the jobs that will be done for you in Hawaii. You've already gotten from the airport in Honolulu to your hotel, where someone checks you in, and another person takes your luggage to your room (which someone has set up specifically for your visit). Time to hit the beach! But before you dash onto the sands, consider all the work that went into building the resort you are visiting. Initially, many people were involved in the decision to build your hotel. This decision, part of what is called "destination development," is a complex process that includes the work of realtors, bankers, market researchers, hotel chains, governments, builders, and many others. Once it was decided to build the hotel, someone had to decide how many tennis courts to build, where to put the swimming pool, how much land to buy, at what price and when, how to deal with local building codes and environmental laws, and how to inform potential customers that a new hotel was being built and what it would offer. And think of all the people in the hotel alone who are working for you: maids, waiters, cooks, front-desk clerks, lifeguards, maintenance people, security guards, and so on. Now have a nice time swimming and sunning, using all the services these people provide.

Tired of the beach? How about driving to the nearby mountains to see the sights? Perhaps your travel agent has already arranged for such a trip. A tour guide might accompany you and tell you about the history or culture of the places you see or point out interesting animals, flowers, and birds. Perhaps you decide to rent a car and strike out on your own. Whatever the tour, each person who supplies you with services is part of the tourist business.

How Travel Developed Throughout History

Your flight to Hawaii could have taken place only in the last century. Before that time, the airplane was not invented, Hawaii was unknown or inaccessible to people in the West, and few Americans had sufficient income or inclination to travel such a long distance.

But people have traveled since humans first decided to change caves. And perhaps the first recorded "tourist" was an Egyptian who chipped his name and the fact that he was away from home on a convenient pyramid in 1500 B.C., thus officially beginning not only a 3,500-year tradition of travel but an equally strong tradition of graffiti.

The ancient Greeks were also travelers, leaving home to attend to business, to participate in festivals, to make pilgrimages, and to see the world. In fact, the Greek writer Herodotus could be considered the first travel writer. He expressed an interest and curiosity about the way foreign people lived. Travel, he felt, was educational.

The Romans adopted all the Greek reasons for travel, and added one of their own: getting away from it all. Well-to-do Romans went "on holiday" to seaside and mountain villas. In addition they visited "ruins" of other great civilizations, particularly the Egyptian and Greek. This led to the development of the support systems needed by tourists—such as inns and guides and interpreters. In the second century, travel to the "seven wonders" of the world was popular. Here was a

"Well, good-bye, dear Mrs. Jones. I hope you will excuse my not having called—the distance, you know! Perhaps you will kindly take this as a visit."

"O, certainly! And perhaps you will kindly take this as a visit returned?"

In the 19th century, travel for vacation purposes become fashionable, but the type of vacation was a far cry from today's.

chance for tourists to see man-made objects, to view the accomplishments of other human beings.

During the Middle Ages, the focus of travel changed again. Instead of going to far-away places for pleasure and curiosity, travelers were motivated by military and religious concerns. The Crusades are an example of this type of travel.

The 18th century saw the advent of the "Grand Tour." Intended for members of the "upper class," the tour was considered a necessary part of each gentleman's or lady's education. It usually included the major capitals on the continent. The young traveler was armed with letters of introduction to both peers and famous personages in each city on the itinerary. The traveler was prepared to "tour" for months or even years. (This explains why the tour was intended for the wealthy; it cost a small fortune.)

In the 19th century, people began traveling for a new reason, to get away from the stress produced by industrialization. Trips to "romantic" landscapes, such as Venice or Greece, became popular.

It was in this century that tourism as we know it was born. Thomas Cook, a teetotaler — that is, a person who abstains from all alcoholic beverages — decided that he could reduce the temptation among the British working class to drink if he took workers on day-long group excursions, thus giving them a break from the humdrum of daily life. In 1841 he organized the first jaunt. The result was a kind of "excursion fever" among the working class. Expansion of the railroad system, and with it the increasing ease of conveyance, meant workers could go farther in faster time. The day-long jaunt stretched to a weekend trip, then in the early 20th century to a week's vacation, as workers won more leisure time as a result of work contracts signed between companies and the new unions.

The excursion moved beyond England and onto the continent, then across the Mediterranean to Egypt. The travel industry formed to meet the needs of the growing number of tourists.

Along with tourism for the masses came the development of guidebooks. The first guide had been written by a Roman in the 2nd century, but the genre did not become common until the 19th century. The new tourist had little sense of what to see and how to behave in foreign environments. Guidebook authors suggested sites to visit and offered a rating system. For example, an author might rank a famous palace on the Grand Canal in Venice as of higher importance to visit than a glassworks factory in the same city. The author also explained the city's customs and suggested rules of behavior so the tourist would not appear to be either rude or a bumpkin.

American travel paralleled the growth of European travel, with the exception, of course, that Americans traveled to Europe to rediscover their cultural heritage. Today, Americans travel to the corners of the earth.

What the Future Holds for Travel

The American travel industry has skyrocketed in the past century, and it is still expanding rapidly for many reasons. For example, nearly half of all Americans today feel that a yearly vacation is a necessity, not just a luxury, and most people have available leisure time. New groups of people now travel, because many of the people who retire earlier have the time, money, and energy to go places. In addition, women are a growing factor in travel, as well as ethnic minority groups that have made economic and social gains that allow more travel. Some analysts even have predicted that travel will be the world's largest industry by the year 2000. This means increasing career opportunities for today's student.

On the other hand, certain events and processes *could* slow travel industry growth or change its direction. One, of course, is the energy crisis. It could continue to cause higher fuel costs that might then raise the price of transportation so much that travel would become very costly. Continuing, unchecked inflation could be a prohibitive factor in the growth of the travel industry. And political problems, wars, and other problems could influence the industry.

On balance, however, the picture is a good one. A student today need only look at the jobs available, examine his or her own skills and interests, and make a choice. Think back to the jobs we talked about during your "Hawaiian vacation." Remember the different levels of work and skills involved — the range of occupations ran from fairly simple tasks that include physical labor (such as baggage handling or food-storage maintenance) or extensive contact with people (such as flight attendant or ticket agent) to more complex tasks in planning and building tourist facilities and services. And don't forget all the behind-the-scenes people working on computers, doing all the business operations entailed in running travel agencies, airlines, and hotels — accountants, managers, clerks, and so on. These jobs can be just as exciting and rewarding as those which are highly visible. Look at the *Travel and Tourism* chart that follows. It shows the branches of the travel industry. Think about the kinds of job you would like to do if you worked in one of them.

We will look at each travel career in more detail later in this book. As we examine careers, ask yourself if you have the skills and personal qualities that are needed to succeed at the job. If you don't have the *basic* requirements and interests for the job, how can you expect to *develop* your skills and talents? Where could a specific job lead if you do it well? Can you make enough money? Meet enough people? Get to travel? All these factors can be important elements in your career decision. The chapters that follow provide some information to help you make that decision about the travel industry.

2
YOUR CAREER AS A TRAVEL AGENT

There are two kinds of travel agencies—wholesale and retail. The retail agency is the most common; its agents make travel arrangements for the general public. The retail agency may be a local, privately owned operation, or it can be just one office of an agency chain. The chain itself may belong to a larger company. In either kind of agency, the travel agent does the same job.

The retail travel agent sells a customer an airline, railroad, or bus ticket, makes hotel reservations, books a cruise, arranges for sightseeing, and even sells travelers' checks and insurance—that is, the agent provides a full range of travel products.

A good travel agent can be more than just a salesperson for travel companies' services and goods. The *professional* agent also acts as a counselor who provides customers with knowledge about destinations, prices, various ways to travel, and the disadvantages and advantages of possible travel alternatives. This agent takes into account peoples' individual differences, their personal tastes in places, climates, recreation, and the like, so as to provide an individually tailored travel package.

The professional agent considers whether an independent or group tour is more suitable for each customer. Does the client plan to take children on the trip who require activities suitable for their age? Or does the client dislike being around children? Perhaps this client would prefer a trip to a quiet and restful

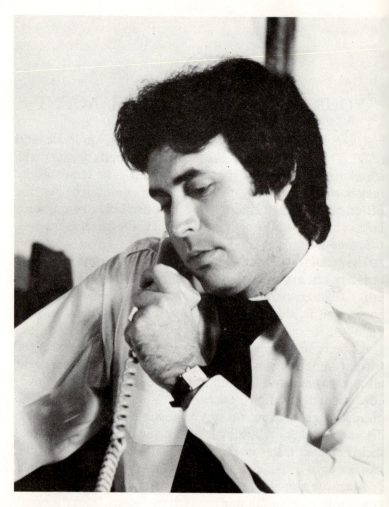

A good travel agent is more than just a salesperson. The professional *agent also acts as a counselor who helps customers tailor a trip to their needs.*

resort. Or does the client long to go "where the action is"? By answering these and many similar questions, the travel agent determines how best to adapt a customer's desires, budget, and available time to a trip that will provide the best travel value and most enjoyment. Remember, the travel agent's job is not only to sell travel products but also, and perhaps most importantly, to provide for the client a reliable and helpful source of *information* about travel.

The Agency Office

Each travel agency office has its own individual look, of course, but some elements are common to almost all of them. Let's say you are planning a trip and drop by a travel agency office in your downtown area.

As you walk in, the office is probably busy with several customers discussing their travel plans with agents who are sitting behind counters or desks. In a nearby corner you probably find a colorful display of brochures and pamphlets that describe tours to lands all over the world. A row of file cabinets lines the walls. These contain many bulletins, letters, and records that agents must have on hand to provide up-to-date, accurate, and complete information for customers. Other file drawers contain the many forms that must be filled out to set up reservations, take out insurance, or record other agency business transactions. Along one wall you see long shelves of reference books. These volumes include schedules and fares and thick atlases containing maps of distant lands. Agents must refer to these books for a multitude of facts and details needed to plan and set up a trip. One of the most commonly used references is *The Official Airline Guide*. This lists airline fares, schedules, and connections to virtually every corner of the world.

You also see a computer terminal. This unit, called a "CRT" (cathode ray tube), displays airline ticket availability on a T.V.-

The CRT is increasingly being used by agents to book travel arrangements.

like screen. The console is directly connected to airlines' computer systems and serves as a kind of airlines' representative in the travel agent's office. This computer terminal, or another CRT you see across the room, may be linked up with reservation systems for hotels, rental cars, and other travel services. Depending on the computer's programming, the console can provide current information on a host of travel topics—weather in cities worldwide, health and passport requirements, the value of foreign currencies, availability of theater tickets in foreign cities, and so forth.

Finally, you notice that there is a telephone on virtually every desk in the office, the telephone is the vital link between the agent and the travel supplier—all those companies that provide the services the agents arrange for their clients.

Basic Skills Needed by a Travel Agent

Your visit to a typical agency office should have given you an idea of the activities that go on there and what you might be asked to do as an agency employee. It also should indicate to you what skills are called for in travel agency posts. If you're interested in working in the travel business, you should:

- Have a good command of basic arithmetic. You will have to calculate fares and commissions accurately.
- Be able to handle detail work. Making travel arrangements means putting together many small elements carefully to make a complete package. Selling a customer a reservation for something as simple as a bus ride from the airport to the city is useless unless you've made sure to make and confirm the reservation and see that it is paid for.
- Be able to communicate well on the telephone. Much of a travel agent's time is spent dealing with clients and suppliers on the phone.

- Be a good salesperson. The travel agent's business is selling services. If you are to succeed as an agent, you must be able to sell the products your agency is offering so that it can stay in business and pay your salary.
- Be able to understand and efficiently use the filing systems, the reference materials, and all the other resources in the office. Remember, the travel agent uses *information* as a prime tool to sell a product. You must be able to put your hands on accurate information rapidly.
- Have a thorough knowledge of geography. You are selling destinations all around the world. Not only do you need to know where places are on the map, what is near them, and how to get to them, but you should have some idea about the climate, political situation, travel attractions, local customs, and so on, for each destination. The more you know, the more information you can supply — and the better your chances of selling a customer good travel arrangements.
- Like people and enjoy dealing with them. You will spend most of your time handling people and solving their problems. If you are uncomfortable around people, if you lack patience and persistence, perhaps this service industry is not for you.

Travel Trainee

Let's assume you like the idea of travel agency work. In addition, you feel that you have the skills and talents appropriate for the job and you find an agency willing to hire and train you. Your agency is called "Star Hunter's Travelogue."

Your first job at Star Hunter's is that of "trainee." This is the "entry-level" position in the agency field — the position usually given to people who are just entering the profession.

As a trainee you will be exposed to all the activities and tasks of the agency so that you can learn what must be done and how to do it. At first, you find this means more clerical work rather than "travel counseling." You are expected to do quite a lot of filing and some typing of correspondence and records. But after a few days, you are typing up itineraries for trips arranged by agents. You have also been asked to deliver tickets to one client's office across the town. By the second week, you find yourself answering phones, directing calls to specific agents, and greeting customers who come to the agency to ask for information or pick up their tickets.

Gradually, you become familiar with ticketing procedures, which are sometimes complex. This is the process of arranging to get the client from point A to point B on time and at the lowest price, then making reservations, figuring out connections, computing costs, confirming reservations, and the like. Eventually, one of the agents shows you how to write tickets and make simple reservations on your own. As soon as you master these tasks, you move on to more complicated work.

Schooling Helps

Besides the on-the-job training we have described, most agencies require at least a high school diploma; a few require some college. An agency might require that you take courses in basic travel counseling either before you join or while you are in training. Such courses are offered by many night schools, trade schools, and community colleges. (See Chapter 9). Even if such a course is not a specific job requirement, it is advisable. It will give you an edge on other candidates seeking jobs in the competitive field.

Because you are new to the trade and because your employer will be training you and perhaps allowing you work time to supplement your training with additional school work, travel trainees make low salaries. Students in travel programs often are willing to work in agencies for little money to get on-the-job experience and to establish contacts with people who might employ them, so there is a great deal of competition even for these low-paying jobs. That is why it is helpful to take courses in the field before you look for that first job. A travel course can help you get your "foot in the door" of an industry that often provides rapid advancement in an exciting career. In a later chapter we'll go into training in more detail.

You as Travel Agent

Imagine that you have gotten some on-the-job experience at Star Hunter's Travelogue, and have taken travel courses to prepare you properly. Now you can become a full-fledged travel agent. Your job is to counsel people who want to travel, to arrange and sell them travel accommodations, and then to make reservations and provide the information needed for a good trip. To do this well, you must deal successfully with *two* different sets of people: your clients and the suppliers of travel products.

Serving the Client

Your first task in dealing with customers is to determine what they want. You must be able to extract from them accurate information about what they want to spend, where they want to go, what they want to do when they get there, how they want to travel, and so on. Often, your customer may be uncertain about the specifics of the trip — particularly if it is a vacation. This client will ask you a lot of questions about possible destinations and arrangements. You must have the information available so that the client can make decisions. You must have this knowledge either in your mind or immediately available in reference books, on the computer console, or by telephone. Your skill in using the resource materials, brochures, and guides mentioned earlier comes into play here, as does your ability to use the company filing system. You should be able to tell your client how to get to the airport and at what time, how much luggage weight is allowed per person and what it will cost if the client has more than the allowable weight, what to wear in Mexico in July or December, and so on through all the details of the travel arrangements.

Using the Supplier

All this information is available from the suppliers of travel products, but you must be able to get them to give you the information quickly and accurately. In some cases the supplier lists the information in a reference book. The following excerpt from a reference flight schedule gives you some idea of how complex these reference works can be. You must know how to read the schedules and rate structures you find there.

You must be able to communicate well with each supplier and understand the products each provides, whether it is a hotel, cruise line, reference book publisher, or official organization. For instance, when you make a reservation at a hotel, you must be sure that the price you quote your customer is correct for the number of people who will stay in the room, the dates of the stay, and the length of the visit. Either a hotel brochure, a standard rate guide, or a hotel reservation clerk can tell you the proper prices, but you must be sure to ask each source the *right* question to get the right answer. Then you must fill out the proper forms, make the proper payments, and make sure the client knows what you have done and at what price.

Pay...While You Go

As a travel agent working in a privately owned, local agency or in a branch office of a larger company, you can expect to make a yearly salary that ranges from $9,000 to $16,000. Although by today's standards this is not very high pay, there is no shortage of people who want to be travel agents. Why? One major reason is the opportunity for low-cost travel.

Low-cost or free travel represents a considerable benefit for travel agents who do not make very high salaries and who must rely heavily on "familiarization" trips to fill out their knowledge of distant locales, transportation facilities, and the like. Many agents work for relatively low pay because they know they will have many chances to travel. But don't assume that being a travel agent means endless free travel and no work. Remember: you cannot sell tickets to your clients while you are cruising the Caribbean. You must be in your office to do that, and you must do it if you want to be paid your salary.

Keeping Up With the Industry

Travel agents also take courses to expand their knowledge and increase their proficiency in many job areas. Airlines, cruise lines, trade associations, colleges, universities, and trade schools offer seminars on a host of subjects relevant to the travel agent's job. There are courses on accounting, office management and efficiency, computer technology, marketing, communication skills, and the like. Taking advantage of these educational opportunities, as well as those offered by travel agent "familiarization" trips, helps the agent do the job better, make more money, and have a better chance to be promoted. (For more information about advanced training in travel, see Chapter 9).

Travel "Specialist"

Up to now we have talked about general travel agencies — often small businesses that deal primarily with a variety of clients who want a mixed bag of travel arrangements, ranging from weekend excursion trips to rather elaborate month-long business trips. Some agencies, however, specialize in serving a particular type of client, and some general agencies are big enough to provide not only the various services we have described but specialized counseling as well. Whatever the business setup, the specialist travel agent concentrates on serving a somewhat narrowly defined group of clients and provides a more narrowly defined product.

One important area of specialization is corporate travel. Many large businesses find it necessary to have some employees travel frequently, over long distances, and for long periods of time. Although a corporate trip can amount to no more than a short hop to company headquarters in the next state, it can also mean the specialist agent is called on to arrange a month-long, round-the-world jaunt for a sales manager. As corporations increasingly expand into collections of businesses located in many countries (so-called *multinational* companies), international business travel has grown. This trend is expected to continue as trade with many countries keeps growing; thus the corporate travel specialist can anticipate rapidly expanding business.

The corporate travel specialist often works under considerable pressure. Business trips are canceled, rearranged, and initiated at the last moment. Business travelers, because they are more frequent travelers and have little time to waste, often are more demanding than general tourist travelers. A business client knows exactly where he or she wants to go, when to get there, and how long to stay. Sometimes a business client even can tell you the airlines, hotels, and other suppliers that the client company or the particular manager wants to use. Your function, with such a well-informed client, is to make reservations for transportation and accommodations as quickly and inexpensively as the client company's standards dictate. The goal here is to get the traveler to the desired destination and back again as efficiently and smoothly as possible.

Another area in which you might specialize is group travel. People everywhere belong to groups. Four of the more important general types of organizations to which many people belong are: churches, community service organizations (the local junior chambers of commerce, for example), fraternal groups (such as the Elks), and hobby or special interest groups. Within each of these categories are hundreds, perhaps even thousands, of smaller, more specific groups. Just think of the organizations that you, your family, and your friends belong to, multiply their number by all the towns, communities, states, and the like in the country, and you will begin to get an idea of how many groups there are. Each of these groups might be interested in traveling together because they share an interest in a place or an activity or just because they get along well together.

The agent who specializes in group travel must possess marketing skills to identify groups and arrange trips that will suit the members' interests, incomes, and experience. The agent also should be especially good at sales. The group travel agent must "sell" a package tour not to a sole client but to a whole series of people who, despite their shared interest, may have somewhat different ideas about where they want to go, how they want to get there, what kind of accommodations and sightseeing they want when they arrive—and what they will pay for it. Finally, the group specialist must have very strong organizational abilities. For example, let's say you're the travel agent who is booking a tour to Rome for 40 Kiwanis. You must book air-charter arrangements for the group, submit the name, address, and phone number of each member of the party, arrange for airport-to-city transportation and for hotel rooms (and, of course, all 40 will want to stay in the same hotel), organize sightseeing, confirm it all, write out ticket form information for each of the 40, and see that payment is received, proper taxes added in, and financial arrangements secured at the Rome end. That is, just the overall picture of such a tour—the actual details are even more involved.

A final example of travel specialization is the agent who adapts travel services to meet the special needs of clients who do not like to travel in groups or on a prearranged tour. They like to travel by themselves on what in the travel industry is called "foreign independent tours" (FITS) or "domestic independent tours" (DITS). The specialist here acts like a tailor who custom fits a suit to the customer. The tailor helps select a fabric, measures the client, directs the cutting and fitting of the garment, makes alterations as needed, and delivers the final product.

Because it is "custom-fitted," the FIT or DIT is often a more expensive vacation that requires a high degree of personal service and involvement from the agent. The independent tour specialist must have extensive knowledge of the area to which the client is going. In fact, this agent sometimes specializes in a particular sort of independent tour, such as photo safaris to Africa, mountaineering expeditions, or visits to archeological sites.

Specialist travel agents must have the same general educational and skill background as general agents. In addition, they must have the specialized knowledge and skills their clients require. This might mean a bit more training in courses or on the job, or simply more years of experience with a particular area of specialization. However the agent acquires the special area of expertise, once he or she has it, relatively higher salaries will follow.

Travel Manager

Let's travel back to the world of your imagination again. Let's say that you have worked for some time at Star Hunter's Travelogue agency as a travel agent and then as a specialist.

You have done an excellent job, and one day the owner asks you to take the position of manager! You're thrilled, and just a little bit afraid. You wonder what you will do as a manager? This depends very much on the size and kind of agency for which you work. Because Star Hunter's is a small, local agency, you will continue to perform some of the duties of a travel agent. In addition, you will be called on to help run the agency, guiding the work of others, training new agents, administering the office, and taking part in the making of business decisions. The larger the agency (or the bigger the company that owns the branch agency), the more complicated and extensive are the jobs the manager might be called on to do. Let's look at some of those jobs in more detail, so that you can decide whether management work in the travel agency business appeals to you.

Running the Office

The manager controls the work of other employees in the office, department, or section. In a small agency this might mean being the boss for only two or three other people, some of whom might be almost as experienced and well-trained as you are. Obviously, in this case the manager shares the responsibility of running the business and the everyday agent tasks we have discussed. In a bigger office or branch the manager directs more people, instructs them on what to do and, if need be, shows them how and when to do it, and so on. Clearly, the manager to some extent is responsible for training the employees, particularly new ones or those who have no experience in a particular area in which the manager has special skills or knowledge.

New Business

Often the manager is charged with bringing in new business to the agency. The manager does this by developing new prod-

cts or ways to sell them, finding new "people markets" in-
rested in buying the agency's products, or improving the ef-
ciency and capabilities of the agency, by installing a com-
uter, for instance.

Administration

Clearly, all these tasks require many different skills, quite a
it of training and experience, and a highly capable and confi-
ent person to do them well. Not everyone has the tact to cor-
ect employees' mistakes without ruffling their feathers, to in-
ill in them enthusiasm for their jobs and willingness to work
ard and well, or to organize a company's total business effi-
iently and profitably. To run the office successfully requires
areful scheduling of work and promotion, skillful balancing
f employees' efforts and hours, and genuine understanding
f the intricacies of accounting, finance, planning, and many
ther aspects of business operations.

Moreover, the manager often must play a big part in organ-
ing, handling, and interpreting the huge amounts of paper-
ork that travel agencies always must deal with. Tickets must
e written, clients must be billed, elaborate sales reports must
e filed with suppliers to correspond to their billing orders,
nd even more complex forms must be filled out for govern-
ent regulatory agencies. Although many travel offices have
ookkeepers and accountants who are responsible for a great
eal of this paperwork, the manager usually has to contribute
good deal of time here as well as supervise the compilation,
ccuracy, and timeliness of all these operations on paper.

More importantly, the manager is responsible for the agen-
y's financial transactions and soundness. The travel office is
n business to make money, after all. It is the manager's job to
ake sure that all the parts of the agency's business mesh
gether to produce a profit. Highly detailed company records
how how well the business is doing and might reveal either

areas of poor management that have to be improved or area
where the business is strong and can grow rapidly. If all th
records are complete and accurate, and if the manager is adep
at interpreting what the records mean, he or she can often sub
stantially increase the agency's business and his or her ow
salary. A special note here: Since much of the recordkeepin
in business these days is done by computers, an agency man
ager must be familiar with these machines and with what the
can contribute to running an agency's operations profitably

Planning for the Future

Let's look at some of the questions a manager will have t
consider and answer in order to make the important decision
that will mean profit or loss for the travel office.

- Who are the agency's customers? Are they local people
  Readers of national magazines?
- Where do they live, and how much money do they spen
  on travel?
- How can the agency's advertising reach more of them
- Can agency employees work more efficiently? Will
  computer help? Does the agency need more employees
  Fewer?
- Are there business or group travelers who need our se
  vices? Can we make more money in this kind of trav
  sale, or should we concentrate on tourist travel by in
  dividuals? Should we specialize in one type of travel
- What will happen to the national economy next year
  State economy? Local economy? How will any of thes
  changes affect our business?

Agency managers generally make between $15,000 an
$25,000 a year. To get these salaries they need extensive e:
perience in the travel agency field, a considerable amount c
training, and personal qualities of intelligence and persistenc

as well as others discussed earlier. As the travel industry becomes more complex, or as managers move from smaller to larger offices, managers need even more education in the complex aspects of managing a business. Indeed, there are many travel managers today who have only high school diplomas. However, the rapid changes we discussed mean that in the future managers increasingly will need to have more advanced education or take extensive advantage of industry-sponsored training in areas such as marketing (discovering groups of people interested in your product and reaching them through advertising), human resource development (training people at all levels in the business, and retraining them as circumstances change), computer usage (for recordkeeping, planning, and decision making), and so on. This means that the future travel agency manager must be willing and able to study hard and expand his or her educational horizons.

Travel Agency Owner

Many agency managers aspire to owning their own business. That way, they make all the decisions about how the business runs and, perhaps, make more money. Such people (and there are a lot of them in the business) both own the business and run it. If the agency is a small business, they often perform the tasks of a travel agent as well. Thus the owner-manager must have all the travel agent skills, plus the manager skills, plus even more ability and willingness to supervise the financial side of the business. The owner must, after all, pay employee salaries, taxes, rent, utilities, and so on. The better the owner-manager runs the business, the more money he or she makes.

We will discuss the problems and potential of owning your own agency in more detail later in this chapter.

The corporate or the wholesale travel agent might arrange travel fo this special interest group of business travelers.

Wholesale Travel Agency

Up to now we have talked only about *retail* travel agencies, although the size and complexity of the agencies varied. Remember that the retail travel office is the one that deals with the general public or business traveler, serving as a link between those who want to travel and those who supply travel facilities. Thus the retail agency sells travel products such as tickets, reservations, tours, and the like.

But who provides the retailer with the products he or she sells? Particularly, who puts together the "package" tours you see described in the many colorful brochures and pamphlets that line travel agency display racks? This is the job of the *wholesale* travel agency. The wholesaler puts together services and facilities that the retailer offers to the public — in other words, the wholesaler assembles the "packages" of travel products the retail agency sells.

Let's look back at the trip you took to Hawaii and examine each role played by the retail and wholesale agents.

The retailer might have contacted all the airlines, hotels, taxis, tour guides, buses, and the like, that you would use on your trip and made separate arrangements with each. (The specialist travel agent often does this.) But chances are that the retail agent sold you a prearranged tour of some kind — one which a wholesale agent had already assembled. The wholesaler combined all the elements into an attractive package designed to satisfy the desires of a great many customers like you and me. How does the wholesaler go about putting together such a package? And what do the traveler, the wholesaler, and the retail agent gain from such efforts?

Why a Wholesaler?

Let's start with the "why" of wholesale travel work. The major advantage of prearranged tour packages is that they can cut costs. The packager — the wholesaler — is often able to buy plane tickets, hotel rooms, and other services at cut rates because he or she is buying larger quantities than the individual retail agent normally does. Remember our example of the tour catering to the specific client just as a custom tailor fitted a suit? Well, the wholesaler operates more like a manufacturer of suits for department stores. The large-scale manufacturer buys cloth in quantities that afford a discount and employs many skilled people who use efficient machines to make "ready-made" suits quickly and at low cost. Customers select a suit that is nearest to their own size and then have the garment altered slightly to fit their particular needs and desires.

The Wholesaler's Operation Benefits Everyone

The travel wholesaler works like the large-scale manufacturer, buying in quantity and putting together a product that meets the general needs of the public. The wholesaler's customers, the retail agents, then sell the packaged tours, which fit people's needs fairly well, although the retailer often alters the tour a bit to make it just right for each customer. The retail agent is able to offer a good product at lower cost, and he or she does not have to spend time making all the arrangements, because the wholesaler has already set them up.

The traveler benefits too. He or she gets a trip for less money and does not have to worry about the details of planning the tour or whether the local agent can find a decent hotel in some faraway place and get the right reservations. The wholesaler has done all that. The brochure the wholesaler provides the retailer tells the agent and the customer just what services are offered and at what price.

Note that the prearranged "package" tour gets its price advantage by the wholesaler's selling a *group* of tickets and reservations. But the tour need not be sold to an "affinity group" of people. In many package tours an individual customer can buy his or her part of the package and make side travel arrangements as he or she pleases, quite independently of anyone else who might have bought the package. Thus the wholesale tour packager serves both the individual and group traveler and, in some cases, even the business traveler, for some packages are designed to meet the needs of corporate executives. The wholesale tour package is a very flexible and useful product.

Packaging of a Wholesaler

Putting together these "packages" is the main task of the wholesale agent. Wholesale agencies tend to be located in large cities, because big cities have more suppliers of the package elements — airlines, major hotels, foreign consulates — as well as better means of communication to reach remote suppliers. Big cities also are an immediate source of large populations (both retail and travel) willing to buy the product.

There are far fewer wholesale agencies than retail ones, just as there are far fewer wholesale clothing manufacturers than there are clothes stores. Many wholesalers concentrate on putting together packages for one area of the world or even for just one country.

Career Opportunities in the Wholesale Market

Jobs in a wholesale agency fall into categories somewhat like those in retail agencies. Beginning or entry-level jobs are mainly clerical — filing, secretarial, and receptionist positions for people with basic office skills. At the next level up a person handles reservations and sales of the packages the wholesaler offers. Initially, reservation and sales personnel record reservations made by retail travel agents on behalf of their clients and make sure that these reservations are processed accurately and promptly. More advanced sales people actively pursue retail travel agent clients, trying to interest them in selling the wholesaler's packages to their individual or group retail customers.

The wholesale agency manager actually puts together the tour packages the agency sells. This skilled job involves planning the routes that a tour will take, making all the necessary purchases of reduced-price tickets, rooms, and the like, and arranging appropriate guides or side tours. Because the wholesaler must resell the services and facilities he or she has packaged to the retailer and still keep the price of the product competitive, the wholesaler does not make much money on any one sale of a piece of the package. The profit comes from volume sales to many customers. Thus the wholesaler is interested in selling many packages to many retailers and individuals. This requires an ability to produce and supervise a great many packages, with all of their many arrangement details.

The wholesaler must be good at handling many things at once and be able to deal with mountains of detail work. Since the wholesaler always tries to get the lowest price on the products he or she wants to package, this kind of agent must be very good at negotiating and bargaining with suppliers — hotels, airlines, cruise ships, and so on. Finally, the wholesaler must have a good sense of the public he or she is attempting to serve, their needs and desires. That is, the wholesaler must be a good marketer.

To land a job as a wholesale tour packager, you must have all the skills of the retailer plus the abilities we outlined earlier — the talent to negotiate with suppliers and the willingness to handle many rather detailed and risky ventures. The additional requirements of the job mean higher salaries than retailers, just as they indicate the need for more experience or training in the field.

Starting Your Own Agency — Some Difficulties and Rewards

Perhaps you have decided that the life of a travel agent appeals to you and, further, believe you can make your *fortune* by opening your own agency. You can't lose, you feel, because you like to travel.

Don't be tempted to open a travel agency just to get a chance to travel a lot at low prices. The industry does offer these opportunities, but the travel agent, like any business person, must be on the job to sell the products, and he or she must be well-informed, skilled, experienced, and well-trained to sell enough products to make an adequate living and stay in business. Time spent on cheap travel usually is not time spent pursuing the important tasks and aims of your business.

Although you may have gathered skills and experience in the industry, perhaps by working for someone else's agency, you will need very specific expertise to start your own travel office.

Ownership Basics

First, you must qualify for "Conference Appointments." This means that in order to sell tickets on airplanes or passenger ships, you must have the approval of airline and steamship associations, or conferences. Transportation suppliers want to make sure that you are financially reliable and that the people in your office know how to write tickets and make reservations properly. They are concerned about this for two reasons:

- Naturally, they want the people selling their products to be competent and honest in general.
- Perhaps more importantly, they have to depend on you, the agent, to set ticket prices correctly and accurately, because they will pay you on the basis of how much you have sold.

The retail agent gets most of his or her income from commissions that suppliers give for selling their services. Thus if an airline gives the agent a commission of, say, 10 percent on the price of each ticket sold, both the agent's income and the airline's profit depend on accurate recording of the ticket price and commission.

The transportation conferences want to make sure that each agency's employees do these jobs properly. To assure that they do, the conference asks that the agency post a bond guaranteeing the operation and the expertise of its people.

The second important need to meet conference standards and, more importantly, to have adequate funds to start up your business is sufficient money (capital). The first year, at least, of a new agency's operation is often not very profitable, so the fledgling agency must have enough money to keep going until it builds up a clientele.

The third and final requirement to start your own agency is good judgment. You must be able to weigh the chance to succeed in your own business against strong competition, frequent changes in the national economy that affect how much the public travels, shifting government regulatory demands, and changing tastes in travel and leisure. You must be able to evaluate the people you hire (or fire) and their contributions to your business. You must be able to decide how much of your own time and energy you are willing to invest in getting the business going and keeping it up. And you must be able to judge whether the high-pressure, fast-paced, but very exciting travel business is for you. In short, do *you* want to enter and can *you* succeed in a generally low-profit industry in order to get the satisfactions of providing personal service, dealing with exotic lands and people, and perhaps doing some traveling yourself?

3
TRAVEL SUPPLIERS: WHAT THEY SELL AND WHO SELLS IT

Many travel industry jobs are with the *suppliers* of travel services rather than with the travel agencies. In fact, this is where *most* of the jobs are. In this chapter and the next three, we will look at some of the jobs available with hotels, airlines, bus companies, railroads, cruise lines, tour-guiding operations, and other travel-related businesses. But first, let's examine several kinds of jobs that all these different employers have in common—reservation, service, and sales agents. These are the people who perform the "public contact" work for transportation, accommodations, and tourist guide companies. By "public contact" we mean simply dealing directly with customers, as do most travel agents.

Reservations Agents

Virtually all segments of the travel industry employ reservations agents. They are the people you talk to on the phone when you call an airline, hotel, or the like, to set up or inquire about transportation or room arrangements. They tell you what flights go where and when they leave and arrive, as well as the fares. They tell how much a rental car will cost and what kinds of cars are available. And, of course, the reservation agent takes and confirms your reservation for the service or facility you want. The reservation agent also sometimes performs the same job for retail or wholesale travel agents, who may call general or special reservation agents to make their arrangements.

Most of the reservation agent's work, if not all of it, is done by phone. He or she spends most of the time wearing a telephone headset, sitting at a computer console that provides up-to-date information on schedules, availability of product, prices, and so forth. The agent also uses the computer to enter reservations in the supplier's system, recording the service or facility to be held, on what dates, the method of payment, special services required, and the like.

Basic Job Requirements

The reservations agent needs a pleasant telephone voice and manner and a great deal of patience to deal with customers' inquiries, complaints, and problems. Since the agent deals with people all day but almost never sees them, it is very important that his or her voice and manner appear cool, calm, helpful. The agent must have an even disposition, a "smile" in his or her voice, and the sense of when to move from providing information to "selling" a customer by taking the reservation. In addition, the agent must be able to type well, and familiarity with using a computer terminal is helpful. Most companies, however, will train you to use a console.

Career Opportunities

Many airlines, and some other travel companies, require that *all* employees begin their careers as "res." agents. Experience, further training, a good res. record, and other factors can lead to promotions to ticketing, sales, and other higher paying and more responsible positions.

Ticket Agents

Ticket agents are employed by transportation and tour-guide companies, in some instances. They sell tickets at bus terminals, train stations, airports, guided tour offices, or

Ticket agents are employed by virtually all transportation and tour-guide companies to make and check travel arrangements.

special offices set up by transportation or tour companies (usually located in big cities) to sell tickets. It is the ticket agent's job to meet people face-to-face, sell them tickets or check tickets issued by travel agents or other ticket offices, weigh and check baggage, tag it to make sure that it goes to its proper destination, assign seats, provide special services for customers, and answer many, many questions. Like reservations agents, ticket agents must be pleasant, helpful, and patient. They, too, do much of their work with computer terminals and should be well versed in computer functions.

Reception Agents

Accommodation companies (hotels, motels, inns, pensions) employ people like ticket agents to receive travelers at their facilities. The reception agent or clerk checks reservations, arranges for payment to be made, routes baggage to rooms, and, again, answers lots of questions. Some hotels and hotel chains make extensive use of computers in assigning rooms and handling other reception clerk functions.

Basic Job Requirements

Reservation and ticket agents, as well as reception personnel, need at least a high school diploma or the equivalent, and some college education is recommended. Because these jobs are public contact work, poise, appearance, and clear and grammatical speech are important.

Career Opportunities

These jobs pay about $12,000 to $18,000 a year and are often considered entry-level prerequisites for employment in the various travel fields. Advancement to supervisory positions is possible, depending on ability, education, and job performance.

Passenger Service Agents

Passenger service agents often are found in railroad stations and at air and bus terminals to help passengers who might have special requirements or problems. These agents help people find the right ticket lines and boarding areas for the correct vehicle. In doing so they answer many questions and must be knowledgeable not only about their own company's services, but about the layout and functioning of the transportation facility in which they work and the area in which it is located. At boarding areas they may be called on to recheck tickets or boarding passes, to inspect international travel documents or customs declarations, to announce departures and boarding procedures, and so on. In addition, passenger service agents help handicapped people, those traveling with small children or pets, the elderly, and others who need assistance in their travel.

Basic Job Requirements

In all their capacities, passenger service agents often are called on to solve a number of minor emergencies and crises during a typical working day. Thus these agents must command not only excellent public contact skills but the ability to think and solve problems quickly. They must instill confidence in passengers and other workers with whom they deal, functioning rather as on-the-spot instant managers who keep all the parts of the company's facilities running smoothly.

Career Opportunities

As more responsible posts than reservation, ticket, and reception agent jobs, passenger service agent jobs pay somewhat higher. They often are "promotional spots" given to agents whom management thinks have supervisory potential. As such, these jobs often are steppingstones to higher jobs.

Sales Agents

To sell their products to the general public or travel agents, travel product suppliers employ many sales representatives.

The sales agent is responsible for maintaining good communications with his or her customers, so that he or she knows what each customer wants to buy and if the customer is satisfied with what they have purchased. For example, a sales agent for a cruise line might contact travel agencies on a regular basis to let them know about new features on certain ships, new ports of call, attractive rates available in special seasons or for special groups, or anything else that might encourage the agents to sell cruises on the company's ships. A sales "rep." for a hotel, on the other hand, might try to get a large organization to hold its annual convention in his or her city and use the hotel's meeting rooms, restaurants, and, of course, private rooms. A sales agent for a bus line might visit a senior citizens' center to talk about short one-day trips to nearby historic sites, or this agent might contact a college alumni group to set up bus travel to the "big game" in the next state.

In short, the sales representative's job is both to get new business and to make sure that current customers are satisfied. Not only does a sales rep. need to know the product thoroughly, but he or she must also understand the market — what can be sold to whom and under what circumstances. The sales agent spends a great deal of time on public relations, making sure that his or her product and services are highly visible to potential customers and keeping his or her ear tuned to developments in the trade and among clients.

Basic Job Requirements

This job requires at least a high school diploma or its equivalent and the ability to sell. In most cases travel sales representatives will have had some other experience in the ravel industry, whether as ticket agents, reception clerks, eservation agents, or in some other job that has exposed them o customers' needs and to the full range of their company's roducts.

Career Opportunities

Successful sales representatives can become sales managers vho supervise other sales agents. As such, they also would levelop marketing and sales strategies for existing and new roducts. Salaries for sales reps. range from $15,000 to 20,000 a year, depending on what is being sold and where. iome companies operate on a commission basis. Managerial alaries are usually considerably higher.

4
JOBS IN TRANSPORTATION

Travel means going somewhere. It requires transportation to carry people from where they are to where they want to go. What kind of jobs are involved in transporting people by car, bus, train, ship, or airplane?

Baggage Handlers

Before a traveler even gets on a vehicle or vessel, the traveler's luggage has to get aboard. Luggage includes everything the traveler is taking — suitcases, skis, tennis rackets, business equipment, or even pets.

Usually, at the entrance to the airport, bus terminal, train station, or ship dock, a person is waiting to assist the traveler in getting the baggage-handling process underway. The *porter* or *skycap* simply may carry your luggage to a check-in counter, or he or she might inspect and weigh it to make sure it meets the carrier's weight and size limits and regulations and tag it for its destination. The destination could be the city where the traveler is going to or just a particular room or facility on a ship. Obviously, it is important that it goes where the traveler goes, no matter how long the trip.

Once the luggage is in the transportation company's hands, someone must get it from the terminal to the vehicle or vessel and see to it that it is properly stowed aboard for the journey. At the end of the trip the process is repeated in reverse: the luggage comes off the vehicle or vessel and must be brought to the transit facility to be picked up by the traveler.

Basic Job Requirements

Baggage handling is considered low-skilled work; therefore people in this profession make low salaries. They do, however get some tips, and there is room to advance to being a super visor of a baggage-handling crew or, perhaps, to managing a company's whole baggage-handling system.

Career Opportunities

Additional training is needed to get and successfully per form these more advanced and better-paying positions. Also driving a baggage-carrying vehicle at a dock, terminal, or air port requires more training and skills. These employees usual ly earn higher pay and their jobs lead to even more demanding and rewarding jobs.

Attendants

Once a traveler passes through the ticket-inspecting and seat-assignment operations and has boarded the vehicle or vessel, the next professional encountered probably will be an attendant. When most people think about "transportation at tendants," they usually think of airplane flight attendants. But all sorts of travel carriers employ stewards and stewardesses on buses, trains, and ships (and sometimes even in fleet vans) to service travel customers and to look after their safety.

Specific details of attendant positions depend on the kind of carrier for which you might work. However, the jobs have general qualities and requirements in common. Let's look at these shared features and then examine in more detail some specific positions that attendants fill.

General Characteristics

The primary quality of a travel attendant is the desire and willingness to be of service to other people. The attendant is

Flight attendants, like other transportation attendants, are concerned primarily with passenger comfort and safety.

called on to answer many, many questions. Sometimes the same questions are repeated over and over: "When will we get there?" "What time is it?" "When do we eat?" and so on. Attendants must know the answers to these questions and be ready to provide the information cheerfully and pleasantly, no matter how many times they are asked the same thing.

Other concerns of the attendant center on the passengers' comfort: handing out pillows and blankets during long trips, helping to quiet noisy children, soothing the nerves of non-related passengers sitting next to the noisy children, pointing out the on-board bathrooms and other facilities, arbitrating disputes about seating arrangements, smoking and non-smoking sections, hand-out equipment for on-board films or music, and so on. And, of course, the attendant serves meals, drinks, and snacks throughout the trip. Here the attendant must work not only efficiently and politely but know how to deal with certain kinds of food and drink in the proper way — for example, how to de-cork and pour wine. Moreover, the attendant must see to it that passengers with special diets or food requirements receive their proper meals.

Finally, the attendant often is responsible for the passengers' safety — to see to it that passengers know about the vehicle's safety equipment, where to find it, and how to use it. Passengers must be told about emergency and routine travel procedures, what to do and whom to follow in case of danger, and even how to behave on board so as not to endanger themselves or their fellow passengers. Often, the attendant's safety function means calming passengers during bad weather, rough travel, or other unsettling moments. Doing this requires tact, calm, and sometimes a strong stomach!

Basic Job Requirements

It is clear from our description that the travel attendant must be a person of great charm and patience. He or she cannot get flustered or angry, since the carrier's continued business with its customers often depends very directly on the impression the attendant makes on the passengers. More importantly, he or she must be able to respond to real or imagined emergencies with the same calm, grace, and tact, since people's lives may well depend on the attendant's decisions and leadership.

A nice appearance as well as a good speaking voice and an easy manner with all sorts of people are other job requirements. Some college education can be a great help in landing one of these jobs, for there is a great deal of competition, mainly because of the chance to travel.

Career Opportunities

Don't expect to make much money at first as an attendant. However, with experience, there are opportunities for promotion to crew chief or manager of attendant operations.

Flight Attendant

In the air, flight attendants perform all the attendant tasks we just described. They must be able to travel on short notice, be willing to spend many nights away from home and family, and be able to perform effectively in the tight and crowded quarters of an airplane.

As mentioned, getting a flight attendant's job is not easy. Many people want the chance to fly, and there are not as many jobs in this field as there once were. This is because the government has decided to "deregulate" the air travel industry. This means that it has decided to relax or remove many of the rules it had imposed on airlines. One result of this has been to lower some air fares. But another result is to eliminate flights on some routes. That means fewer miles flown with fewer flight attendants needed to work the flights. Another factor in the decline in air attendant jobs has been the energy crisis, which has contributed to the reduction of the number of flights flown on many major airlines.

If you are fortunate enough to get hired as an attendant trainee by an airline, you will spend four to six weeks learning your job at the airline's training center. You will be taught emergency procedures, public contact skills, food and beverage service, grooming, and other aspects of the attendant's job.

Once you have begun to work as a flight attendant, you will be eligible for many low-cost or free trips that are made available by airlines to their own employees and those of other airlines. This kind of travel is one of the major benefits in a career that does not pay exceptionally well.

Basic Job Requirements

Obviously, flight attendants must be cordial, neat, and enjoy caring for people's needs. Pay for flight attendants ranges between $9,000 and $17,000. The higher salaries go to those with special skills, for instance, the ability to speak a foreign language. These attendants work on flights going outside the United States and must assist large numbers of people who don't speak English. The higher salaries go also to those who work for certain higher paying lines, or who are willing to put in considerable amounts of overtime.

Career Opportunities

Promotions in the field of flight attending are possible. You might become an in-flight supervisor, responsible for the work of a flight attendant crew. On a jumbo jet this can mean coordinating and supervising the activities of 15 or 20 people. Or you might move into management of ground arrangements for flight services, including catering (food and beverage services), marketing, administration, or training. All these more advanced positions require four years of college education or even graduate study in business or airline operations.

Crew

Every vehicle or vessel is driven, piloted, guided, or serviced during its trip by its crew. The "crew" might amount to no more than a bus driver who operates all the systems on the vehicle alone and simply follows interstate or local highways to the destination. Or crew might mean an airplane crew consisting of pilot, copilot, and navigator, with all the special skills needed to operate a giant jet plane. Or the crew can be that of a ship, with its captain, mates, engineers, and hands doing various jobs to keep an enormous ocean liner working and on course.

Basic Job Requirements

Needless to say, each of these jobs requires very special training and lots of experience. One good source for such training is the armed forces: many pilots are trained in the Air Force; ship personnel often come from the Navy; and some drivers get their first experience with big vehicles in the Army. College training and industry programs also are available to prepare you for these jobs.

Career Opportunities

Crew salaries and opportunities vary tremendously, with bus drivers making as little as $10,000 a year on local routes, and commercial airline pilots and ship's captains earning up to and over $100,000 annually, including benefits and overtime.

If you want to find out more about some of these jobs, see your guidance counselor, look into military service training, or read about these industries in your school library. ARCO's *Your Career in the Airline Industry* can also tell you a great deal about crew jobs in transportation.

Maintenance

Travel transportation equipment must be serviced and maintained. This requires the work of skilled auto and bus mechanics, train, plane, and ship maintenance personnel and engineers, and clean-up and supply crews.

Basic Requirements and Opportunities

Again, the range of positions and salaries is large, depending on the kind of vehicle or vessel serviced, experience, training, location, and so on. And again there are many sources of information about such jobs that you can find at your school or in your community. Just keep in mind the variety of maintenance positions available in the travel industry, what your chances are of getting one, and how you might go about doing it.

5
ACCOMMODATIONS JOBS

Whenever you travel, you have to have a place to sleep and eat. The tasks entailed in providing you a place to sleep and food to eat are "accommodations" jobs. Perhaps this is the travel field where you will make your career.

Usually, we think of accommodations in terms of hotels or motels and the restaurants in them or nearby. But cruise ships provide all the same services and facilities in a compact setting. So we will examine accommodations careers as they appear on board ship. That way, it's easier to view accommodations in detail.

Think of a cruise ship as a kind of floating hotel. To begin to get some idea of the range of accommodations jobs available, look at the calendar of a typical day on board a ship.

6:30 am	Eye-opener coffee is served	Promenade
7:45 am	Breakfast is served (main seating)	Dining Room
9:00 am	Breakfast is served (late seating)	Dining Room
9:00 am	Slot machines open	Casino
9:30 am	For the physically "pfft" — exercises and deck hike	Sun Deck
10:00 am	Coffee, rolls & bouillon	Lido Deck
10:30 am	The Shore Excusion Office is open for sale of tour tickets	Forward
10:30-11:15 am	Your cruise staff will be available to help you with materials and ideas for the Crazy Hat & Masquerade Party	Showplace

10:45 am	Learn to "Do the Hustle" with Debbie	Mardi Gras Club
11:15 am	Ports-of-call briefing with the Cruise Director	Showplace
Noon	Luncheon is served (main seating)	Dining Room
Noon-3:00 pm	Complimentary hamburgers & hot dogs	Lido Deck
12:30-1:30 pm	Fun and games in the sun	Pool Deck
1:30 pm	Luncheon is served (late seating)	Dining Room
2:00 pm	Current feature length movie (Movie repeated at 4, 6 and 8 pm)	Cinema
2:00-3:00 pm	Horseracing "Daily Double"	Showplace
2:00-3:00 pm	Calypso music	Poolside
2:30 pm	Trapshooting	Upper Deck, Aft
2:30 pm	Bridge Tournament begins	Riverboat Club
2:40 pm	Games available (Scrabble, Password, Chess)	Promenade
3:00 pm	Grandmother's Bragging Party	Mardi Gras Club
3:30 pm	Visit to ship's bridge (please meet promptly at the Purser's Office at 3:30 pm)	Purser's Office
3:45 pm	Plank Jousts	Poolside
4:00 pm	Tea is served	Lido Deck
5:15 pm	Musical cocktail time	Riverboat Lounge
6:00 pm	Dinner is served (main seating)	Dining Room
7:00 pm	Full Gambling Casino opens — Try your luck!	Casino
7:15 pm	Musical cocktail time	Riverboat Lounge
8:00 pm	Dinner is served (late seating)	Dining Room
8:30 pm	Dancing to the tunes of Mark V	Mardi Gras Club
9:00 pm	It's Jackpot Bingo Time for mountains of money $$$	Showplace

10:00 pm	Registration for the Crazy Hat and Masquerade Party	Riverboat Lounge
10:30 pm	The Crazy Hat & Masquerade Party begins	Showplace
12:00 'til...	"The Good Time" entertains into the "whee" hours	Fly-Aweigh Disco
12:15 am	MIDNIGHT SPECIAL Cabaret Show featuring Harold Wand	Mardi Gras Club
12:30 am	Midnight Buffet is served	Dining Room
1:30 am	Late Night Buffet is served	Promenade
2:00 am	Fly-Aweigh and Casino still going strong	

That's quite a list! Let's pick out of it the kinds of jobs required.

Food Preparation Jobs

First, there are jobs related to food preparation. Notice how many meals are served — in fact, the kitchen and dining room staffs must be ready day and night to feed the passengers, providing full meals in the ship's restaurants, snacks and drinks in various activity areas, and food service for passengers' staterooms. There must be cheers who plan and cook all these meals, kitchen helpers to do less-skilled tasks, clean-up people to maintain the kitchens and their equipment, and food servers, including the waiters in the dining rooms, and stewards to bring food and drink to staterooms, decks and so forth

In addition, dieticians are needed to consider nutrition and the ordering of supplies, and wine stewards must select and buy beverages for the voyage, as well as offer them to passengers. Butchers, bakers, pot and plate washers, moppers and cleaners, and even menu writers and printers — all must get involved to ensure that the food service is superlative.

Whether on shipboard or at a resort or hotel, guests are assured of having good times by a myriad of personnel, from grounds attendants to cooks and recreation specialists.

Recreation Specialists

Next there are recreation and activity personnel. (We will talk about cruise directors and their jobs in more detail in Chapter 6.) Note here that all the "social" activities on the ship require planning, execution, and large staffs to gather, organize and provide people with the proper facilities and equipment to enjoy themselves. Somebody has to buy decks of cards and put them on tables for people to play with, just as someone orders records and spins them at the disco. And somebody has to clean up after the party.

Stewards and Maids

Third, there are people concerned with the comfort of passengers in their rooms. They include stewards and maids, who provide room service and see to it that the rooms are in proper condition.

Behind-the-Scenes Staff

Finally, the behind-the-scenes staff maintains and services the whole ship. Besides the crew, charged with keeping the ship running and on course, there are laundry personnel, who provide clean sheets, tablecloths, napkins, and even clothes for crew and passengers; maintenance personnel, who make sure that the plumbing, lighting, air conditioning, phones, radios, and the like work; and cleaners, who work throughout the vessel to keep the ship tidy and in order. The ship might also have barbers and beauticians, masseurs and athletic trainers, doctors and nurses, entertainers and librarians, as well as communications specialists to send your telegrams, calls, or letters to shore.

What's Needed To Go Sailing?

The cruise ship operates much like a tiny society or community that tries to provide its visitors with all the services and facilities necessary to make their stay enjoyable. (Large resort hotels operate in much the same way.) In doing so it employs literally thousands of people to do hundreds of different jobs. If you have or can develop any of the skills mentioned (and more that you can spot by examining the ship's daily calendar carefully) you could probably work in a big hotel or on a cruise ship—or in the same job in your home town.

6
GUIDES AND DIRECTORS

We noted in the chapter on travel agencies that people increasingly travel in groups. Whether the group is formed around special interests, common destinations, or simply the urge to save money by buying in volume, the group is today a common and growing factor in the travel business.

One feature that sometimes attracts travelers to group tours is the presence of a "guide," someone who accompanies the group throughout the tour and handles many of the details of its travel arrangements. The guide or escort's main job is to see that everything runs smoothly during the trip.

To see just what "everything" can mean, let's look at a day or two in the life of a typical escort bringing a group from New York to London.

All Aboard for London

The escort will probably meet the group for the first time at New York's international airport. His or her primary duties during this initial period are twofold and illustrate well the essence of the guide's position. Basically, it is his or her job to be sure that all the many, many details involved with the flight are handled properly for each individual member of the group and for the group as a whole. First, the guide makes sure that all the travelers are present and that their tickets, baggage, seats, and other needed transportation arrangements are in order. Since this is an international flight, the guide also helps the group members with passports, customs declarations and inspections, and currency exchange questions and problems.

Second, in the course of ensuring that arrangements are in order and people are securely on the flight, the escort begins to get to know the group members he or she will be helping throughout the tour—which could last as long as several months, but probably will run for two or three weeks. It is very important that the guide have a sense of who the passengers are, what they like and dislike, which people in the group get along well together and which do not. The escort relies on this information to see that the personal arrangements of the trip also go well—that each individual member of the group has a pleasant, trouble-free journey. That way, the group as a whole enjoys itself.

During the flight, the escort continues to function as group envoy: following up on special arrangements for tour members, finding out about clients' preferences and interests, and providing information and aid about upcoming arrival procedures that can confuse and disturb people after a long seven-or eight-hour flight. Again, passports, customs and health declarations, and currency exchange matters are uppermost in people's minds, and the escort must be ready to cheerfully and knowledgeably repeat the same information over and over to people who might be on their first trip abroad and therefore are worried about every aspect of the trip.

London by Day and by Night

Upon arrival in London, the escort leads the group through the maze of customs and baggage procedures, keeping the group members together through gentle cajoling and calls for patience at this slow point in the trip—tourists are always so eager to get going! The guide then loads the group and their baggage into buses or limousines, making sure to note who sits in back and who in front, which members like to stay together and which ought not to be near each other, and who in the

A tour escort must be patient, cheerful, knowledgeable, and ready to work long hours.

group might need the guide's special help or support during later flights or rides. The escort must keep track of these matters throughout the trip so that no one feels slighted in terms of getting the best seat in the bus, having a chance to sit near friends, or missing the escort's tour information because he or she was sitting too far away to hear.

At the hotel the escort leads the clients through check-in and baggage distribution, making sure that the right luggage goes promptly to the right room. The guide also reminds everyone about the next activity, in this case a half-day bus tour of London to get the group familiar with the main sites and layout of the city. The escort might post reminders and announcements on a special bulletin board, along with times and seating arrangements for meals, notes about special places to visit or shop, and so on.

The guide performs the same jobs at each stop on the trip — checking on details of arrangements, answering questions about schedules, money, and the like, and dealing with minor and major emergencies. After all, the escort is also fully responsible for the group's health, happiness, and welfare throughout the trip.

Basic Job Requirements

This sketch of an escort's work shows quite clearly that the job demands a person able and willing to deal with people of all sorts. A guide must be patient, cheerful, knowledgeable, and ready to work long hours. Additionally, the escort must be intimately familiar with the customs and practices of the locale the group is visiting, including the language of the host country as well as the language the group is most comfortable with speaking. All U.S. tourists are not necessarily most comfortable speaking in English. And all tours are not sponsored by U.S. companies. Tour group members might speak Chinese, Spanish, Japanese, or Hindustani. As more and more foreign travelers come to the United States, demand for multilingual group escorts in this country is growing.

Career Opportunities

Pay for this demanding job is fairly low, although the escort's salary is often supplemented, and sometimes quite substantially, by tips and gratuities from tour members. An obvious benefit of the job is the opportunity to travel to places the escort otherwise might not be able to visit. But remember that the tour escort's job is not touring—he or she usually is lucky to find as much as an hour a day to spend privately.

Sightseeing and Tour Guide

Let's go back to our imaginary group touring London. Let's assume that the escort has been successful at getting everyone and everything organized: members have eaten, rested in their rooms, and are now assembled, ready to go on a half-day bus tour of London. For many tour members, this is the first time they have seen the city.

This tour bus has a guide to introduce group members to various London sites and attractions and to explain to them what they are seeing and what they should be on the lookout for. The guide is an expert on the tour area—someone who knows intimately the history, art, architecture, customs, and the like, of each attraction. The guide is paid to interest tourists in the city's features by educating and entertaining them.

On the London bus tour, the female tour guide points out attractions to group members, explains what is important about each site, and adds hints on how to enhance enjoyment of visiting it and other points after the tour has ended. To hold members' attention, she tells several amusing or tantalizing anecdotes about a building barely glimpsed, paintings to be enjoyed in a local museum, or the delights of dining in some special or out of the way place.

Basic Job Requirements

Guides usually live in the countries and cities that they describe. Outside the United States, most guides are multilingual, so that they can handle groups from many parts of the world. As the United States becomes a more attractive tourist destination for foreigners, the need for multilingual guides here is increasing.

Like escorts, guides must like to be with people, must have a good command of their descriptive material, must not mind answering questions, and must not get bored with repeating the same tour information.

Career Opportunities

Pay for guides is not high, and the job is usually seasonal. Most locales have slack and peak periods for tourism during the year. However, tips can be substantial, particularly if the guide works either for an individual tourist or for a very large group. In some cases the guide also is the driver of the tour vehicle.

Cruise or Resort Social Director

If the group travels to a resort or takes a cruise, the travelers will run into a person with another kind of job geared to ensuring that group members have a good time — the social director.

Gone are the days of the old fashioned "cruise director." The stereotype was an endlessly cheerful person who always said "Everyone out for shuffleboard."

Today's social director must have much more of a sense of people's individual tastes and needs, as well as fine organizational skills to deal with large groups, big ships, and enormous resort complexes. It is his or her job to provide a wide variety of entertainment and activities that will appeal to all passengers or guests. And the director must be able to sense when people are too shy to get involved in something they really want to do or, on the other hand, when they genuinely want to keep to themselves. Being a social director might be as simple as finding a fourth person for a game of bridge, or as complicated as planning a reception or party with the catering or kitchen staff. It might mean organizing volleyball teams, or just making sure that guests stay happy at what they are doing or not doing.

Basic Job Requirements

In many ways a social director has to have the same skills as a successful party-giver — basically, the ability to get the right people together at the right time to do the right things in the right atmosphere. If *you* can put people at ease, and get them to mix well and have a good time, you probably would make a good social director.

Career Opportunities

The social director needs a high school diploma. The ability to speak a foreign language is definitely a plus. A pleasant personal appearance and friendliness are obvious attributes that potential employers look for in hiring social directors.

7
OTHER CAREERS IN TRAVEL — AT A GLANCE

So far, we have looked in detail at the most visible kinds of jobs in the travel industry — travel agents who arrange trips and sell tickets, the suppliers of travel packages and services, and people who work for transportation, accommodation, or touring companies.

Now let's look a little more behind the scenes. Who sets up the travel supply companies in the first place? Where do they get the research data on the kinds of facilities and services needed? What kinds of people make the suppliers' very important and costly decisions? Who trains travel people? And finally, who circulates travel information, both to people within the broad area covered by the "travel" industry and to the general public?

Let's start with "tourism planning" — the process of deciding where to build travel facilities, the kind of setup needed, how to finance it, and who should work in it.

Tourism Planning

We have talked about travel to various destinations for various purposes without considering how the destinations got there. How does a place originate or become popular with travelers?

Obviously, many major tourist spots come into being and grow in popularity with travelers without people in the travel industry making any concrete efforts to popularize the sites. For example, the major cities of the world are all among the most important tourist and business traveling destinations.

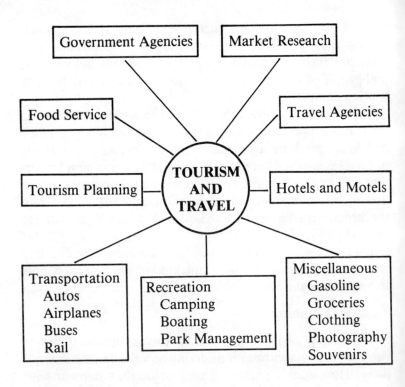

The "travel" industry is composed of numerous specialties and auxiliary fields of business.

Their attractions are obvious. People throughout history have been drawn to the great cities, with their multitude of goods, variety of people, collections of national and cultural treasures, and concentration of interesting events on the political, business, sports, musical, and theatrical stages.

No tourism planning has ever been required to make Paris or New York or Tokyo a "natural" travel destination. As they evolved, these cities supplied what was needed to attract and maintain visitors. What did require thought and planning, however, is the location and design of facilities to meet varying needs of travelers.

Consider the following business traveler to New York. This financial executive wants to get to her destination quickly and efficiently, stay in reasonable comfort for one night at moderate price, and have access to the people she wants to meet. Since she is to do business on "Wall Street," as the financial district is called, she wants to stay near the southern end of the city. The facility that will suit her needs best will be quite different from the one that will meet the needs of another person whose business takes him to Westchester County, some 40 miles north of Wall Street. This businessman also is accompanied by his wife, who plans to tour New York while her husband works. The couple views their trip as a chance both to see the city and do business there. Their needs are different from the executive who plans a one-day work stopover downtown, and the tourism facilities planned for each stay are different. One requires a simple hotel room situated within easy reach of downtown, and the other needs a centrally located facility, with easy access to midtown shopping areas and, preferably, with entertainment. Someone must be aware of the needs and desires of the variety of people who come to major "natural" attractions, and must plan and build an appropriate set of accommodations, travel services, and tour operations to attract their business. This is tourism planning in its simple form.

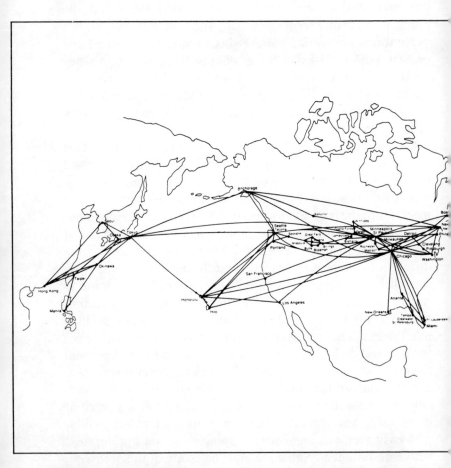

The government of each nation determines what airlines and other modes of transportation can come into and go out of its dominion.

At the other extreme is the totally undeveloped destination, one that in its natural state has little to offer the visitor. Imagine a broad expanse of sandy, white beach shaded by towering palms and washed by gentle, warm surf. The nearby forest is filled with exotic animals and birds, easy to spot and fun to watch at leisure. The "locals" are friendly, hospitable people, skilled in many crafts, producing colorful and inexpensive clothes and trinkets. The ocean is filled with beautiful coral formations and plenty of small and large fish, good for sport and snorkling or scuba excursions. Fresh water is abundant, as is tasty native food of various kinds. What is missing, from the travel industry's point of view? A way to get tourists to the site, publicity to inform potential visitors of the spot's attractions, a resort hotel, and the related facilities.

Let's look at the process of building a hotel complex in this imaginary paradise to see who is involved in the decision and what has to be decided.

Accessibility

Perhaps the first question to be answered is, "Can people get to this place?" Planners must consider not only the location of an airport, but other aspects of transportation as well, such as the availability of local taxis or buses to get large numbers of tourists from planes, trains, or ships to the hotel. Are there good roads? Are there roads at all? Are there people willing and able to work as taxi or bus drivers? Do any locals have the mechanical and organizational skills needed to run a local transport business and money enough to buy the right kind of vehicles? Can the local companies provide sufficient work so employees can make a living?

Government Involvement

Will the government of this unspoiled paradise welcome the development of tourism — will government representatives

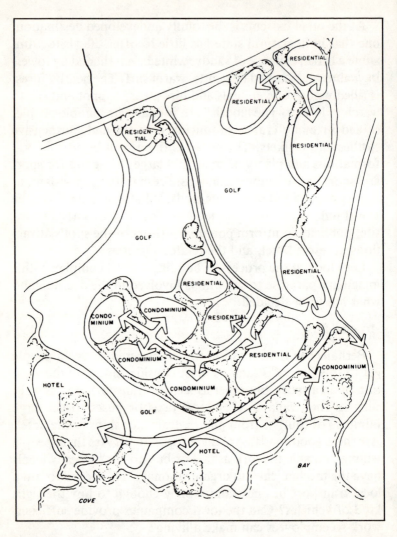

Resorts don't just happen; someone must plan the location and facilities.

make this part of their country accessible to foreigners?

"Foreigners," in this case, might mean somebody from just a few miles away. The government might be a local U.S. body, for instance. The people in charge must decide what impact tourism will have on their locale and how much freedom from outside interference the locale is willing to give up to make the kind of money that comes from the development of a tourist facility and the services that go along with it.

Other issues that the host government might raise include the effect the development will have on both the human and the natural environment. Will visitors change for the good or bad the way in which the local people live? What will happen to local crafts and customs when the natives are exposed to different ways of living? Will visitors who hunt and fish in the local forest and ocean kill too many animals, fish, and birds? Can the local animal population even stand to have more humans near their habitats without giving up their lairs or nests? What effect will the concentration of large numbers of people have on the food supply and garbage disposal systems of the area? These and even more details must be sorted out.

Who Are Tourism Planners?

Who answers all these questions? Travel and tourism planners do, and in the course of their work they employ many people to look into specific aspects of the questions they must answer. There are architects and builders who plan and construct the facility itself. There are researchers who look into the environmental, cultural, and political questions raised by the planned development. There are skilled negotiators and lobbyists who work with government agencies and legislatures to achieve the developers' goals. And there are financial and business analysts who examine and develop sources of money and personnel for the project.

Career Opportunities

The careers of all these people require a fair degree of experience and education. Moreover, many of them work with firms that are not considered directly part of the travel industry. However, if you are interested in this aspect of travel work, you should plan on developing a strong educational background in the field that interests you, as well as accumulating the required years of experience. Then you should seek out a building or research or accounting firm that specializes in travel-related work. You can plan on making a good salary, but you will have to put in substantial time and effort in training and gaining experience before you do.

Market Researcher

Our imaginary beachfront paradise appears to be the perfect setting for a resort hotel development, just as it seems quite clear that New York or Tokyo should have hotels to meet the various needs of travelers. But other destinations with lesser attractions or problems with accessibility and adequate facilities are harder for travel industry representatives to decide about in terms of building facilities or supplying services. For instance, what if a resort is already on the unspoiled beach we described? Is there room for another? We are not talking here about the physical space needed to put up a building, but the business space required of the locale if it is to support another facility. Can the new facility attract tourists in sufficient numbers to make the investment in a new hotel worthwhile? Will a new airline or route going to this new development be profitable? Would a new steamship company or route be more profitable?

Answering such questions is the job of the travel market researcher. The main responsibility of this person is to find out how interested people are in visiting a locale, what kind of facility they want to find when they get there, and how they want to travel. Moreover, it is the market researcher's job to determine the kind of people who will take the trip: Will they be wealthy retired couples from the United States or Europe? Will the place attract young singles interested in meeting people and having a good time? How much money will they have to spend and on what? Will the region or hotel draw a lot of people from one racial or ethnic group? Will this group expect or require any special considerations or arrangements, such as special dietary restrictions?

The developer of a tourist facility relies heavily on market research. Since the developer must decide just what to build and where, and what services to provide at what price, he or she must have accurate market studies based on the latest information and statistical techniques.

The market researcher must be able to set up a study of large groups of potential customers, design and administer questionnaires that reveal how people feel about a destination or tour package, and then analyze the questionnaire results.

Basic Job Requirements

Skills needed by a market researcher include mathematics and computer use at a rather sophisticated level, the ability to interview people and design questionnaires, and the know-how to set up, execute, and report on one's study.

College and graduate programs in this field are a necessity.

Career Opportunities

Entry-level positions in market research pay well and often lead quickly to promotion.

Trainers

Let's assume that market research has determined that a resort would do well if it were set up on our imaginary beach.

Now the buildings and facilities have been designed, constructed, decorated, landscaped, equipped, and so on, and the resort is ready to open. But who will train the people who are to work there in their skills? This is where trainers come in.

Trainers usually have some background in the skill they are to teach as well as a familiarity with the techniques of specialized, rapid education. Some large companies employ full-time trainers, but many hire trainers on a free-lance basis to train personnel in one job at one time.

Trainers teach skills that range from rather complex accounting or financial procedures to the ability to cook or serve food at a hotel restaurant table.

Most airlines have large training departments for pilots, flight attendants, ticket agents, telephone representatives, and even other trainers. Some bus, train, and cruise lines maintain similar facilities. And many companies specialize in certain skills or industry segments that provide freelance trainers to customers in the travel field, as well as outside it.

Basic Job Requirements

Trainers usually have a college degree in human resources or in a training specialty and often have graduate training as well. It is not unusual to find former school teachers in the training field, as well as people who have held a variety of positions in a specialty and are now imparting the skills they gained to others.

Career Opportunities

Pay is good as a trainer, as are opportunities for advancement, business-related travel, and other benefits.

Travel Writer

Perhaps you admire and envy the writers whose work appears in glossy travel magazines or the travel sections of local newspapers. They have the chance to travel and then write about their experiences for money. "I wish I could have that job," you think. "But I could never get a job like that."

All travel writing is not limited to these rather glamorous and highly paid positions. There are a multitude of writing jobs in the travel industry that are more modest in their requirements, rewards, and purposes.

Remember the many brochures and pamphlets you saw lining the wall of Star Hunter's travel office? Someone had to write the "copy" or information that filled those pamphlets — the glowing descriptions of the tours or destinations and the more down-to-earth, detailed sections on rates, dates, and places available. And someone "wrote" or compiled the information for the big schedule and fare reference books that the travel agent uses to provide accurate and up-to-date information on trains, planes, buses, and ships. Everything in the travel field that is in print, in fact, has to be written by someone: guide books and schedule sheets, feature articles in magazines, hotel rules and regulations, newspaper reports, and restaurant menus — all require writers, editors, or production editors with varying degrees of knowledge, experience, and skill.

Basic Job Requirements

If you write well and enjoy putting words on paper, you might consider travel writing at some level. The better you are, the more willing you are to hone your skills through training and work experience, the more chance you have to move up from schedule compilation to, perhaps, a glamorous job working for a big travel magazine.

The main requirement to get an entry-level job in the writing field is a very good knowledge of English grammar. Courses or extracurricular work on your high school newspaper as a writer or editor also will contribute to your ability to get a job in the field. Most writers do, however, have a college education.

You might start work as a secretary or assistant at a travel publication. With luck and ability you might be promoted to copywriter for some routine and fact-filled part of the publication—say, writing up the "How To Get There" part of an article on visiting Hawaii, in which you list the airlines that fly there, rates, schedules, and so on. The next step up might be a short article or part of a feature, and then could come a job as a full-time writer. Many travel writers also work freelance, handling one assignment at a time for a variety of publications.

In addition to publications that inform the general public about the travel industry or tourism in general, there are many "trade" magazines that publish information about travel that will interest primarily those people who work in the industry. These publications range from magazines that deal with the industry as a whole to journals, bulletins, newsletters, and the like, that report on special aspects of tourism and travel. There is a variety of specialized publications about resorts, motels, airlines, travel agencies, specific markets or groups of people who travel, and various destinations. Jobs with "trade" publications might be less visible to the public and thus less glamorous, but they often pay very well and involve a great deal of free travel for the writer.

Career Opportunities

Travel writing as a career can involve great rewards in terms of pay and the chance to travel. But the field is very competitive at the higher levels and rather volatile—people change jobs rapidly and frequently, sometimes under less than friendly circumstances. So you must be prepared to compete, to move with opportunities, to face insecurity, to see what is coming and decide what to do about it. Most importantly, and obviously, you must be able to write well.

8
APPLYING FOR A JOB

Before you fill out an application for a job or go for an interview, you first must decide what kind of job to apply for.

Let's start this difficult task by trying to plan the kind of career you would like to have, say, five or ten years from now. The three forms that follow will help you do this kind of planning and self-examination. First, we have supplied a filled-in sample of each form to show you the *kind* of information requested. A blank form follows the sample. Use a duplicating machine to copy each blank form, or copy out each form by hand on blank paper. Then take as much time as you need to think about the questions and fill in the blanks accurately and honestly. Remember that you are testing yourself and your aspirations for the future, so be thorough and honest with yourself. If you find it hard to fill in many of the blanks, you may need more information. One source is people in the field who are willing to talk to you. Try calling up a local travel agency and asking an agent some questions about salaries, experience, education required, and so on. Another good source of information is the guidance and career counselor in your school. He or she often can answer some of your questions or direct you to where to look. Your school or public library also will have books that can give you further information.

On the next page is a sample form on "Long-Term Goals" with the blanks filled in to give you an idea of how one person planning a career might answer the questions.

Long-Term Goals
Sample Form

In five years I want to: *manage a travel agency*

In order to achieve this goal I need:

Education (level): *probably some college courses*

Education (subjects needed): *accounting*
marketing
personnel mangemen

Experience (jobs held): *travel agent or*
trainee / ticket
agent ?

Experience (in years): *3-5*

Personal qualities and skills: *ability to handle*
details, ability
to sell, a
liking for people.

Applying for a Job

Money to invest?	Yes ☐	No ☑
Will this be a good job to have in five years?	Yes ☑	No ☐
For salary?	Yes ☑	No ☐
For potential advancement?	Yes ☑	No ☐

I think I'll need extra $. Maybe a college course will teach me about financing.

Can I get the skills or develop the personal qualities needed?   Yes ☑   No ☐

How? *I have to find out if I can get money for some college courses.*

Can I afford more school?   Yes ☐   No ☑
Can I get financial help for school?   Yes ☐   No ☐ ?

Why do I want this career, and is this reason realistic?

I want to travel, but if I manage an agency, that's a lot of hard work. Will I have the time to travel? Who can tell me?

O.K. Now that you have an idea of how to fill out the form, fill in your own personal long-term goals. Write the questions on a blank piece of paper or duplicate the blank form that follows. Now fill out the form.

Long-Term Goals

In five years I want to: _____
_____

In order to achieve this goal I need:

Education (level): _____

Education (subjects needed): _____

_____

_____

_____

_____

_____

Experience (jobs held): _____

_____

_____

_____

_____

Experience (in years):_____

Personal qualities and skills: _____

_____

_____

_____

_____

Money to invest?	Yes ☐	No ☐
Will this be a good job to have in five years?	Yes ☐	No ☐
For salary?	Yes ☐	No ☐
For potential advancement?	Yes ☐	No ☐

_____

_____

_____

_____

Can I get the skills or develop the personal qualities

   needed?   Yes ☐   No ☐

How? _____

_____

_____

_____

_____

Can I afford more school?   Yes ☐   No ☐

Can I get financial help for school?   Yes ☐   No ☐

Why do I want this career, and is this reason realistic?

_____

_____

_____

_____

_____

Answering the questions on this form about the somewhat distant future should have led you to think about the present and about the more immediate future—the next few years. Put aside your plan for the future for now to concentrate on where you are at the moment.

The next form on "Self-Assessment" will help you to pinpoint what you do well, what you have to offer to an employer, and what you do poorly—those areas that need to be worked on or improved. It will also give you some sense of your likes and dislikes.

Turn to the sample form on the next page. Look it over, then fill out the copy of the blank Self-Assessment form you have made from the blank form. Feel free to add skill areas or questions that pertain to your situation. The important thing is to write down what is true for you and what will help you to evaluate and develop *your* career plans.

Plan to work on the form for several days, since you will need time to think over your first responses, perhaps revise your views, and explore additional sources of information about yourself, such as school records, guidance reports, or the opinions of trusted, honest teachers and acquaintances. It is very hard to do this kind of self-evaluation quickly or at one sitting. Again, your school guidance counselor probably can help you out here by showing you how to answer some questions about yourself, by giving you similar but larger inventories or forms for self-assessment, or by sharing his or her own skills and experience.

**Self-Assessment
Sample Form**

WHAT SKILLS DO I HAVE?
(List below what you do **well**.)

Office equipment: *I can type 40 words per minute and use an adding machine.*

Mathematics: *I liked basic math and got good grades. I took some advanced courses.*

Speaking: *I like to talk to people and have a pleasant speaking voice.*

Spelling: *I got good grades.*

Reading: *My English teacher says I read about the 10th grade level.*

Penmanship: *I have neat handwriting.*

Composition: *I get good grades on my papers.*

Getting along with people: *I get along with my friends and adults.*

Working with people: *I work with others pretty well.*

Other abilities I have: *I like to be the boss.*

WHAT AREAS AM I WEAK IN?
(List below what you do **poorly**.)

(Any of the categories from the skills list might appear
here, if you have trouble with any of those items. And,
of course, you can add whatever else gives you trouble.
For example, you might feel that "I don't like to work
with others very much.")

*I like to work with others as long as
I'm the boss. When someone else
is running the show I always think
I can do it better. and my
friends say I'm too domineering.*

LIKES AND DISLIKES
(List below those things you feel fairly strongly about that
might relate to your job.)

Likes	*Dislikes*
Talking on the phone	*Lots of noise*
	Being bossed around
	Regular hours

Now fill in your copy of the form. What skills, likes, and
dislikes do you *really* have?

Applying for a Job

Self-Assessment

WHAT SKILLS DO I HAVE?
(List below what you do **well**.)

Office equipment: _____

_____

Mathematics: _____

_____

Speaking: _____

_____

Spelling: _____

_____

Reading: _____

_____

Penmanship: _____

_____

Composition: _____

_____

Getting along with people: _____

_____

Working with people: _____

_____

Other abilities I have: _____

_____

WHAT AREAS AM I WEAK IN?
(List below what you do **poorly**.)

(Any of the categories from the skills list might appear
here, if you have trouble with any of those items. And,
of course, you can add whatever else gives you trouble.
For example, you might feel that "I don't like to work
with others very much.")

_____

_____

_____

_____

_____

_____

_____

LIKES AND DISLIKES
(List below those things you feel fairly strongly about that
might relate to your job.)

Likes	*Dislikes*
_____	_____
_____	_____
_____	_____
_____	_____
_____	_____
_____	_____

Filling out this "Self-Assessment" form should help you evaluate the personal skills and qualities you have or lack for that future job. More importantly, it will help you to decide on the kind of *first* job, or entry-level position you want to seek in order to get started on the pursuit of your long-term goal.

Now that you have filled out copies of two forms, you should be familiar with the kind of thinking and research you need to do. Briefly look over the "Entry-Level Job Sample Form," and then fill out a copy of the blank form. Make a copy of the form, and fill it in to see what your entry-level job requirements will be for your *first* job. For example, you may have decided the first job you might be able to get on the long road to owning your own travel agency is that of "travel agent trainee." You would then fill in the qualities and experience you would probably need to land such a job.

Fill in the blanks on your copy of the following form to find out if the entry-level job you have in mind will help you to attain your long-term goals. (You may wish to fill out the form using different kinds of entry-level jobs or other variables, such as adding or subtracting additional school or financial help.)

Entry-Level Job
Sample Form

My immediate job goal is: *travel agent trainee*

In order to achieve this goal I need:

Education (level): *a high school diploma*

Education (subjects needed): *probably some college too. But typing in high school will help, and accounting and shorthand.*

Experience (jobs held): *Fox's Landscaping (summers)*

Experience (in years): *2*

Personal qualities and skills: *Like people and have a pleasant speaking voice. I'm polite.*

Money to invest?	Yes ☐	No ☑
Will this be a good job to have in five years?	Yes ☑	No ☐
For salary?	Yes ☑	No ☐
For potential advancement?	Yes ☑	No ☐

_____

_____

_____

_____

Can I get the skills or develop the personal qualities
needed?   Yes ☐   No ☐

How? _Maybe I should contact an_
agency and see what else would give
me an "edge" when I go for a
trainee's job.

_____

Can I afford more school?   Yes ☐   No ☑
Can I get financial help for school?   **?** Yes ☐   No ☐
Why do I want this career, and is this reason realistic?
To travel.

_____

_____

_____

_____

Entry-Level Job

My immediate job goal is: _____

_____

In order to achieve this goal I need:

Education (level): _____

Education (subjects needed): _____

_____

_____

_____

_____

_____

Experience (jobs held): _____

_____

_____

_____

_____

_____

Experience (in years):_____

Personal qualities and skills: _____

_____

_____

_____

_____

Money to invest?   Yes ☐   No ☐

Will this be a good job to have in five years?   Yes ☐   No ☐

   For salary?   Yes ☐   No ☐

   For potential advancement?   Yes ☐   No ☐

_____

_____

_____

_____

Can I get the skills or develop the personal qualities

   needed?   Yes ☐   No ☐

How? _____

_____

_____

_____

_____

Can I afford more school?   Yes ☐   No ☐

Can I get financial help for school?   Yes ☐   No ☐

Why do I want this career, and is this reason realistic?

_____

_____

_____

_____

_____

Both the "Long-Term Goals" and the "Entry-Level Job" forms have areas to list your personal skills and weaknesses. You can fill in these qualities from the answers you get on your "Self-Evaluation" form.

Now put all three forms side by side. What do you see? Answer the following questions to help you decide whether your skills and goals match:

- Do I *now* have the necessary skills to get my entry-level job?
- If not, what will I have to do to get them? Can I afford to do so in terms of time and money? Will I need a job while I prepare?
- Does my long-term goal make sense? Do I have time and money to do what I want to do in five years? In ten years?

At this point you may well have to change either your immediate job goal, your eventual career choice and plan, or both. If you don't have the skills and qualities necessary for the job you want now and the one you want ten years from now, then you must take an honest look at yourself and decide if you can develop the necessary abilities and talents. And you must think about whether this effort will be worth the trouble, considering the kind of career it will eventually lead to. Will the long-term goal job pay you enough money to own your own house and support a family? Are either of these important to you? Will you really get a chance to travel? Are there further opportunities for advancement and growth in this field?

If the answers on your forms do not match up well with your goals, you should fill in the forms again, using different immediate and long-term goals. But if you find that your skills fit well with what you want to do, then you are ready to make your first approach to a potential employer.

Writing a Letter of Application

You might see an advertisement listing a job you want in the newspaper, or you might plan simply to write "cold" to a travel agency in your town asking for a job. But no matter how you locate a job opening, you then must apply for the job.

Your letter of application is the first contact you probably will have with the company or person who might hire you. The letter must be a good one if the company's personnel director or the travel agency's owner-manager is going to notice it and not just toss it in the wastebasket. So work hard on making the letter a good one, and remember that lots of other people are doing the same thing for the same job.

The application letter is often called a "cover" letter, because you attach it to your resume (which we will discuss in just a moment) to explain why the prospective employer should consider you for the job. The cover letter is the attention-getting part of your application.

Needless to say, your letter will get plenty of attention if it is messy, hard to read, or badly spelled — but it will be the wrong kind of attention! Your letter must be:

- Typed in standard business-letter format
- Grammatically correct
- Free of spelling errors
- Within the rules of good composition and expression.

The application letter should be short — no longer than one typewritten page. It should state what you are applying for and summarize very briefly the major skills and qualities you have that you think qualify you for the job.

Find out who will look at your application, and address that person directly rather than beginning the letter with "Dear Sir" or "Dear Madam." You often can find out who will read your application by calling the firm you are applying to and asking,

```
                                        45 Oak Lane
                                        Anytown, Kansas 98765
                                        (507-555-1212)

                                        November 23, 1981

Mr. John Jones
XYZ Travel Agency
123 Main Street
Anytown, Kansas  94321

Dear Mr. Jones:

I am interested in applying for the position of trainee
with the XYZ Travel Agency.

I believe that I meet the general requirements for the
position. I am currently completing a course in airline
ticket writing, and have the ability to relate well to
other people, a good command of both written and
spoken English, and experience with handling work that
involves a lot of detail.

I type and know how to operate the Apollo Reservation
system and an adding machine.

I have attached a resume of my education and job experience.

I would appreciate an opportunity to file an application
and talk with you about how I can put my skills to work
for the XYZ Travel Agency.

                                        Very truly yours,


                                        Susan Smith
```

Sample Letter of Application

"I want to write to the person responsible for hiring at your company. Can you give me the person's name, please, and how to spell it?" Be sure to spell the person's name correctly!

Here is a sample letter for an entry-level travel job:

The Resume

Your resume summarizes your education and experience — it is a kind of self-portrait. Along with the cover letter, it is meant to interest a potential employer, show him or her what you have to offer, and lead to an interview. When you prepare your resume, keep in mind the employer who will read it, and try to supply him or her with as much relevant information about you in as brief a manner as possible.

Outline your skills, talents, experience, and so on, and devise a format that shows each of these elements clearly to the person who will read your application. Remember that "experience" need not be *job* experience: if you have applicable experience in school, in extracurricular activities, or even at home that shows your accomplishments and potential, then list it in your resume.

The trick in writing either a cover letter or a resume is to think carefully about what you want to portray as your capabilities and what your potential employer wants to see in you as a possible worker. Write the resume to emphasize points that probably fit well with company needs and expectations.

Your resume should be neatly typed, with no grammatical, spelling, or typing errors. It should be no more than one page long, unless you have had considerable work experience. Here is an imaginary resume made up for Susan Smith who is applying to XYZ Travel:

Notice how this resume points up the work that Susan has done, the courses she has taken, the awards she has gotten,

```
                        Susan Smith
                        45 Oak Lane
                        Anytown, Kansas 98765
                        (507-555-1212)


    EDUCATION:   1981. Acme Travel School, Anytown, Kansas.
                 Courses in airline ticket writing and using
                 automated reservations systems.

                 1977-81. Central High School, Anytown, Kansas.
                 Graduated in the top quarter of class.

    EXPERIENCE:  1978-80.  Assistant bookkeeper and clerk,
                 Anytown General Store.  Duties included totaling
                 day's receipts, keeping inventory records, waiting
                 on customers.

    AWARDS AND   George Smith Award at Central High for best
    ACTIVITIES:  four-year average in business classes.

                 1978.  Treasurer of International Relations Club,
                 Central High.

                 1979.  President of International Relations Club,
                 Central High.

    REFERENCES:  Contact Bob Brown, manager Anytown General Store.
```

Sample Resume

and the activities she has pursued that are related to work she may do for the people at XYZ Travel. She might have listed winning a cookie-baking award, but what relevance would this have to her potential employer? None, of course. Make sure you don't clutter up your resume with pointless information.

The Interview

The interview is your chance to sell yourself face to face to your prospective employer. Obviously, you want to make the best possible impression, including looking your best. So dress conservatively, in tailored clothes, and make sure you are well groomed and on time for your appointment.

It is just as important to prepare yourself mentally for the interview. This means finding out something about the company to which you are applying. Ask people in the neighborhood if they know anything about the business, read whatever you can find about that firm in particular or about the industry in general, and talk to your school guidance counselor. He or she might have pertinent information. In addition, think through what you plan to say about your experience and skills and why you want to work in the company and in the industry.

The person who interviews you is looking for someone who will fit in the structure of the company and who will contribute to achieving its goals. He or she needs to find out if that is you. To do so, the interviewer might take one of several approaches. The interviewer might recognize that you, like most applicants, are very nervous, and he or she might try to put you at ease and draw out your best qualities through gentle questioning. But the interviewer is just as likely to try to see how you react to pressure by "putting you on the spot" with hard questions. In either case, you will do best in the interview if you try to anticipate the interviewer's techniques and questions and rehearse your answers and the way you will handle whatever the interviewer does or says. Practice your responses and be alert. Most important, know what skills and talents you have to offer and be confident about them and yourself.

Also remember that the interview is a chance for you to find out some things about the company to which you are applying and to decide whether it is a place you would like to work. You will probably be given a chance to ask questions, so be prepared to do so. This not only gives you an opportunity to learn about the firm, but also provides a chance to display your interest in the company, its products, and its services.

Center your questions on defining exactly what your responsibilities, duties, hours, and pay will be, along with possible questions on "fringe benefits," such as insurance, a tuition-refund program to cover the cost of relevant courses, and so forth. Also use the interview to fill in the blanks that remain in your picture of the agency's business. Inquire, for instance, about the firm's areas of specialization, plans for growth, and the like.

The interview often ends with the interviewer telling you a date by which you can expect a decision. If he or she does not volunteer this information, be sure to ask for it. If you are offered a job on the spot but want time to think about it, you might say something like, "I'm certainly interested, but I have another interview tomorrow. I can let you know right after that."

If you are lucky enough to be offered more than one job, your decision may be difficult. You may have to weigh higher pay offered by one firm against what you may see as the opportunity to learn and advance more quickly in another position. This is where all that hard thinking you did about your immediate and long-term goals should come in handy. Look back at the forms that outline your goals and how to meet them. Which job appears more likely to advance you toward those goals?

Personal Contacts and Job Hunting

It is sometimes said that "It's not what you know but who you know" that is important in landing a job. This is certainly not always true. But if you have any contacts, this is the time to turn that contact into an advantage in looking for a job.

In the business world, and elsewhere, a great deal of business is done by calling on people you know to do things for you. In turn, they call on you. Once you get your first job, you will have a chance to make the kinds of contacts that later will be valuable to you. But even in looking for your first job, you may have contacts that you can call on: your guidance counselor at school, your parents and their friends, your friends' parents, people who have employed you part-time, or who have worked with you – all these people know other people who might be able to help you in your job hunting. Let them know what kind of job you are looking for, what your aims, talents, and goals are. Give them a chance to help you, and many of them will, for quite a few people get real pleasure from helping young people get started in their careers. This is especially true if the young person can instill in these contacts confidence in his or her maturity and reliability.

The Follow-Up

After your interview it is always a good idea to write to the interviewer to thank him or her for the interview and to remind the person of who you are and what you can do. Here is Susan's letter.

```
                                         45 Oak Lane
                                         Anytown, Kansas 98765
                                         (507-555-1212)

                                         November 30, 1981


Mr. John Jones
XYZ Travel Agency
123 Main Street
Anytown, Kansas 94321


Dear Mr. Jones:

Thank you for the opportunity to talk with you yesterday
about the position of trainee at XYZ Travel.  I enjoyed
meeting you and learning about the agency.  Since your
agency has recently purchased a computer-ticketing system,
I believe my course work in automated reservations systems
will be particularly valuable to XYZ Travel, as will my
two years' successful experience in dealing with the public.

I look forward to hearing from you.


                                         Sincerely,

                                         Susan Smith
```

Sample Thank You Letter

9
EDUCATION BEYOND HIGH SCHOOL

Throughout this book we have mentioned travel courses that can help you gain skills and learn about the industry. Let's look now in more detail at what these courses offer, where you can find them, and how important they might be for your career advancement.

Employers' Requirements

How much value prospective employers in the travel industry place on education beyond high school varies greatly with the company and with the segment of the industry to which you are applying for work.

Some firms feel that it is very important for new employees to have a grasp of at least the basic information and skills needed to do the job when they are hired. Other companies feel that such training is wasted until the new employee has worked awhile and knows what further training is required for the job he or she has been hired to do. They prefer that training go on while the new employee works. Yet other businesses believe that the only worthwhile training comes from doing the job. The only way to be certain what a prospective employer wants in the way of training is to ask.

Where to Find Training

There are many paths you can follow to find training in travel after high school graduation. Here are the most important sources of courses:

Schools

For many careers in the travel industry, you are most likely to find the courses you need at trade schools or community colleges in your area. You may, in some instances, take just a few courses, often at night. But some colleges also offer associate degrees in travel agency skills and management. Such degrees usually are earned in two years of study.

For more ambitious goals, such as a planned career in managerial or specialized travel positions, a four-year college degree in business administration or some similar field is more appropriate. Many college programs offer majors in travel specialties, as well as more general business skills. Certain universities offer even more advanced courses at the graduate level.

A convenient guide to college offerings can be found in *Lovejoy's College Guide.* Here is an abbreviated list of some programs:

Northern Arizona University	Office of Admissions Box 4103 Flagstaff, AZ 86011	Lodging, Tourism, Restaurant
Canada College	Admissions Office 420 Farm Hill Rd. Redwood City, CA 94061	Associate degree, tourism
Fullerton College	Admissions Office 321 E. Chapman Ave. Fullerton, CA 92634	Associate, travel agency management
Metropolitan State	HMTA Department Box 60, 1006 11th St. Denver, CO 80204	B.A., travel administration
University of New Haven	Admissions Office West Haven, CT 06516	Associate, B.A., major in tourism and travel administration

George Washington University	Travel and Tourism Programs 817 23rd Street Washington, DC 20052	B.A., M.A.
Florida International University	Admissions and Records Office Tamiami Campus Miami, FL 33199	B.S., hospitality, travel and tourism
University of Hawaii	School of Travel Industry Management College of Business Honolulu, HI 96882	B.A., M.B.A.
Parks College of St. Louis University	Institute of Transportation, Travel & Tourism Cahokia, IL	B.S., major in transportation, travel and tourism
Iowa State	Admissions Office Beardshaer Hall Ames, IA 50010	Major in transportation
Bay Path Junior College	Admissions Office Longmeadow, MA 01106	Associate degree, travel and tourism
Ferris State College	Admissions Office Big Rapids, MI 49307	B.S., hospitality management, travel and tourism
St. Louis Community College	Admissions Office 5600 Oakland Ave. St. Louis, MO 63110	Associate degree
Adelphi University	Admissions Office School of Business Garden City, NY 11530	B.A., major in transportation, travel and tourism

Genesee Community College	Director of Admissions College Rd. Batavia, NY	Associate degree, travel agency management, tour guides
ASTA Travel Course	Education and Training Dept. American Society of Travel Agents 711 Fifth Avenue New York, NY 10022	Basic skills course for travel agents
New School for Social Research	Graduate School of Management and Urban Professions 66 Fifth Avenue New York, NY 10011	B.A., M.P.S.
Niagara University	Admissions Office New York, NY 14109	Transportation, travel agency operation
Johnson and Wales College	Admissions Office Abbott Park Place Providence, RI 02903	Associate degree
Edmonds Community College	Admissions Office 2000 68th Ave. West Lynnwood, WA 98036	Associate degree

Before you select any program, investigate it thoroughly. Study involves a large investment of your time and money, so be sure that your choice is right for you. In choosing a school, talk to school representatives or alumni about your career goals and how the school's programs can help you achieve them. Look at the courses offered and compare the skills they will give you with those required to meet your immediate and long-term plans. Use the forms you filled out to guide your evaluation of a school's programs.

"Alumni," people who have graduated from or attended a school you are interested in, are a good source of information. Ask them if they got what they wanted and needed from the school. Prospective travel employers are another good source of information about schools that offer travel training.

If you are planning to enter a trade school, be sure to check out the school's reputation with the state department of education where you live as well as with the Better Business Bureau. Representatives of these institutions can tell you if the school is properly licensed and reliable. They might even be able to tell you about the school's record in placing its graduates in jobs.

No reputable school can *guarantee* you a job when you complete its program, but it can help in your job hunting by providing you with good placement service. Evaluate a school's placement service by asking how many graduates have gotten jobs and the kinds of jobs they have gotten. Compare the school's placement record with your goals and make sure that its program will start you in the direction you want.

Industry Training Programs

Many industry sources offer training workshops, seminars, or courses for travel agency employees. The airlines, for example, run courses in advanced ticketing procedures (stressing computer console work), interpreting fare schedules and tariffs, developing sales skills on the phone and face to face, and using automated equipment. Cruise lines offer similar seminars to increase agents' product knowledge. Some of these "courses" are, in fact, very attractive cruises, during which agents study ship facilities and procedures.

Several trade associations provide workshops and seminars for their members. They include ASTA (the American Society of Travel Agents) and ARTA (the Association of Retail Travel Agents). Working agents also can get courses from ICTA, the

Institute of Certified Travel Agents. ICTA offers a series of courses that takes about two years to complete. A person who passes the ICTA examinations becomes a Certified Travel Counselor, or CTC. The ICTA courses include business management, marketing, sales management, and domestic and international tourism. Note that many travel agencies and industry suppliers will pay for at least part of their employees' training in any of these programs.

Correspondence Courses

If you cannot afford the time or money for school or industry training programs, or if you live where such training is not readily available, you should consider taking one or more of the various correspondence courses that are available.

The American Society of Travel Agents (ASTA) offers one such course. It includes 14 lessons and a final examination. The student studies the material, in booklet form, and completes a test for each lesson. The test is mailed to ASTA headquarters, graded by a qualified travel agent, and returned with comments. The course covers: introduction to the travel agency, geography, international and domestic ticketing, railroads, motorcoaches, cruises, hotels, car rental, automation, and selling skills. You may obtain information about the ASTA Travel Course by writing: Education and Training Department, American Society of Travel Agents, 711 Fifth Avenue, New York, New York 10022.

Another course is offered by Trans World Airlines. Called the "Home Study Course for Selling Travel," it consists of 18 lessons. The subjects covered are similar to those in the ASTA course, but more emphasis is placed on automation. Both courses have tests and grant a diploma. For information on the TWA program, write: Trans World Travel College, Breech Academy, 6300 Lamar Avenue, Overland Park, Kansas 66201.

AFTERWORD

Do you feel there is a future in the travel business for you? There is if:

- You genuinely like people and like to be of service.
- You have good communication skills.
- You can handle detail well.
- You are willing to accept a salary scale somewhat lower than that in other businesses in exchange for the fringe benefit of low-cost or free traveling.
- You can accept and even welcome a rapidly changing business environment.

REFERENCES

The ASTA Travel Course
  The American Society of Travel Agents
  711 Fifth Avenue
  New York, New York 10022

Guide to Buying, Selling, and Starting a Travel Agency
  Laurence Stevens
  Morton House Publishing Company
  8 South Michigan Avenue
  Chicago, Illinois 60603

Lovejoy's College Guide
  Simon & Schuster Publishing Inc.
  1230 Avenue of the Americas
  New York, New York 10020

The Official Guide to Airline Careers
  Alexander C. Morton
  International Publishing Company of Miami
  665 LaVilla Drive
  Miami Springs, Florida 33166

The Official Guide to Travel Agents and Travel Careers
  Same as above

The Tourist Business
  Donald E. Lundberg
  CBI Publishing Company, Inc.
  51 Sleeper Street
  Boston, Massachusetts

INDEX